If you mention pizza to an Italian or samba to a Brazilian they will know instantly what you mean and it is the same if you say origami to the Japanese, they understand immediately that you are talking about the art of paperfolding. They might even be so flattered by your interest in the subject that they would give you some tips on the craft. They may probably even fold a crane bird for you, which is the traditional Japanese model that many Japanese people can fold. However, just as nowadays pizza and the samba are not confined to their country of origin, origami is found not only in Japan but has also been introduced into many countries.

● If you are interested in finding out more about the history of paperfolding, you will come across two different traditions, that are believed to have developed independently of each other: an Asiatic tradition with Chinese–Japanese origins and a European tradition which originated in Spain. The craft of origami as we know it today in the West began in the early 1950s in England, and contacts with Japan for a deeper knowledge of the art soon inspired others to form a network of enthusiastic and creative paperfolders in Britain, the United States and Europe.

● Since I became deeply interested in the craft of origami, I have discovered that it involves not only folded paper figures but also the personalities and nimble fingers of their originators. ● I have traveled through many countries trying to trace these people and, in this book, I will present some of the models I came across during my trips.

● Folding brings opportunities for unfolding!

Paulo Mulatinho

Paulo Mulatinho

Origami

30-Fold-by-Fold
Projects

CHARTWELL
BOOKS. INC.

Contents

What do I need for origami?

The answer is simple: just paper!

You can find paper just about anywhere in many different qualities and sizes. You can use any type of paper you like as long as it can be folded. One-colored or multicolored, thick or thin, smooth or rough, expensive or cheap, large or small — it all depends on your taste and the model you want to make. You can use gift wrapping-paper, drawing-paper, writing-paper, parcel wrapping-paper, paper used for handicrafts, and so on. The only disadvantage of these types of papers is that you first have to cut them to the correct starting size for your model — in most cases a square, sometimes 11.6 x 8.25 in (29.7 x 21 cm). If you want to save yourself this chore, you should buy origami paper which comes in a square and is ideal for folding. Your local stationery or handicrafts shop will probably have a selection. I take a little pack of origami paper with me everywhere and am ready to start folding whenever the occasion presents itself.

Symbols

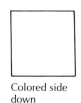

Colored side down   Colored side up

 Fold forward and backward

 Turn over the model

 The following drawing is shown to a larger scale

 Open out the model at this point and fold it in the direction shown

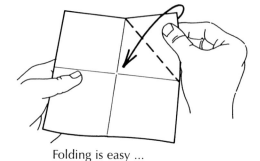

Folding is easy ...

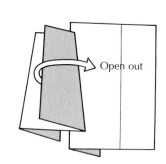

In the following instructions you will find all the information you need for folding a model set out in the form of drawings. Lines and arrows tell you what to do. Each of these internationally accepted symbols has its own meaning and is explained here. In the instructions themselves I have only added explanatory text where I considered it helpful, or to point out stages where things may possibly go wrong. Each individual step shows which fold should be made. The result of this fold is shown in the following drawing for the next step.

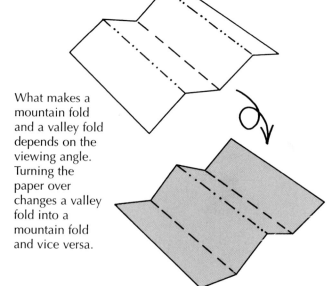

What makes a mountain fold and a valley fold depends on the viewing angle. Turning the paper over changes a valley fold into a mountain fold and vice versa.

The instructions in this book, with the mountain and valley folds and the different types of arrows, constitute a kind of "language" between you and me: you would like to fold the model shown and I would like to explain the folding sequence to you by means of the drawings. Since we cannot hold a "true" dialogue, I hope that as few misunderstandings as possible will arise between us. However, if any do, the fault is certainly mine. I do realize that a set of instructions cannot be perfectly clear to everyone.

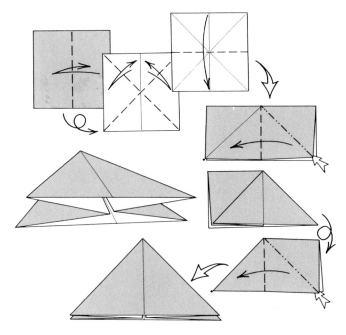

This is called the waterbomb base ...

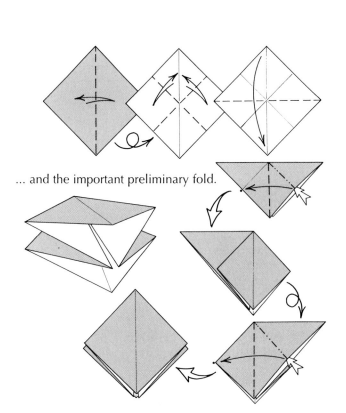

... and the important preliminary fold.

Beginners especially, who are not that familiar with the rather technical drawings, can easily get stuck during the folding, each one in a different place. Worrying over it just does not help. Put the paper aside, do something else for a while, and at a second attempt you will probably get the hang of it immediately. Do not worry about making mistakes, they can lead you to your goal.

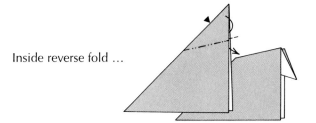

Inside reverse fold ...

Simple
and
Amazing Models

Envelope

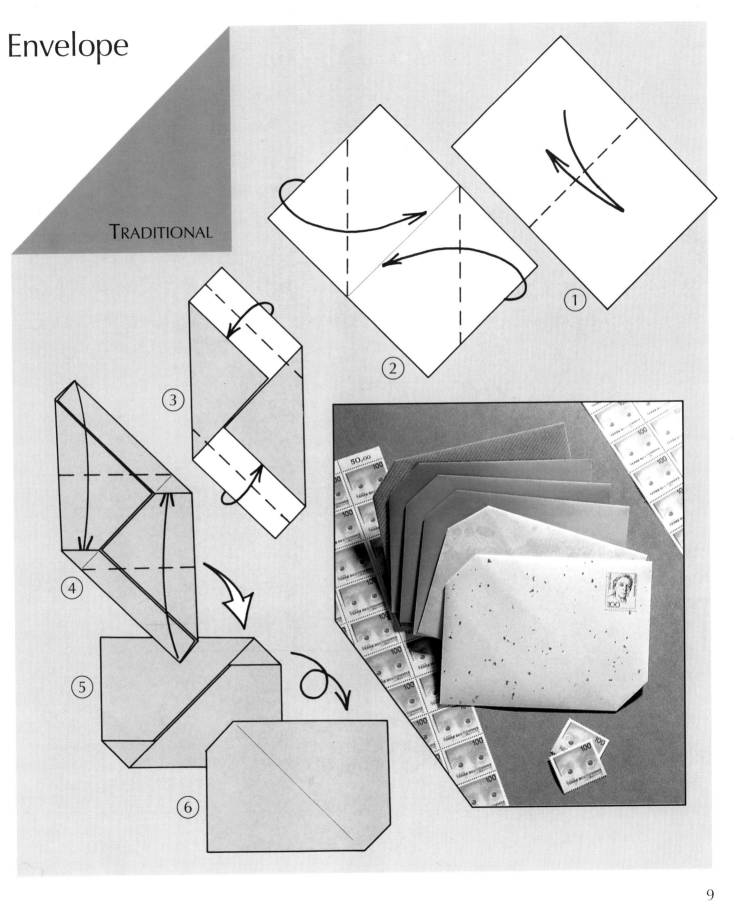

① ② ③ ④ ⑤ ⑥

Crossed
Box Pleat

THOKI YENN

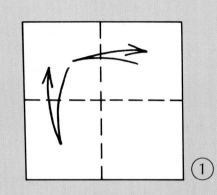

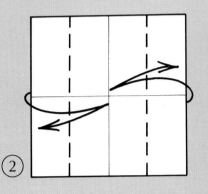

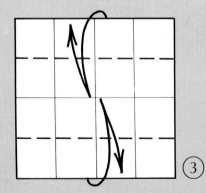

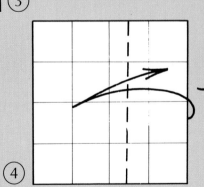

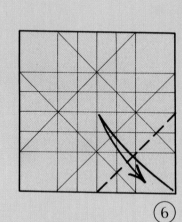

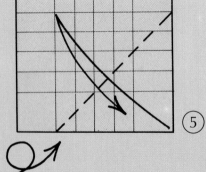

Repeat the folds shown in
steps 4, 5 and 6 with the
other three edges and
corners respectively.

No new creases are being made in step 8, but the existing mountain as well as valley folds have to be creased again sharply. This will make it easier to push the parts together in the next steps.

⑧

⑦

⑨ When pushing the edges together, make sure that the mountain and valley folds correspond to the ones in the drawing. Turn the model over after you have stressed the relief.

⑩

⑪

Push the parts together in the center and flatten the upstanding parts to the side.

⑫

Seen from the bottom.

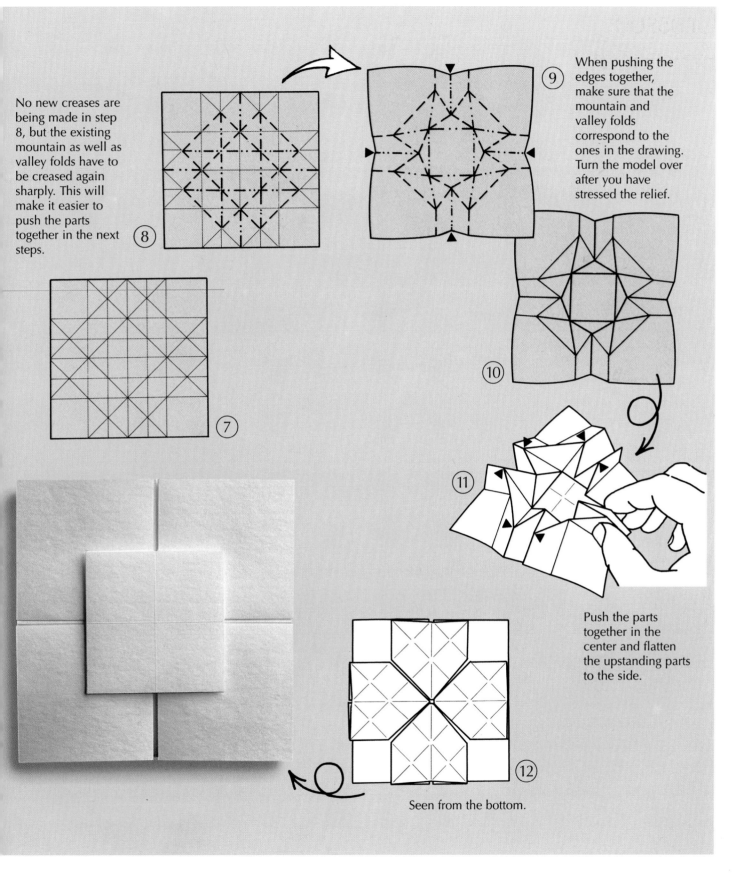

Nose and
Mustache

Gabriel Alvarez

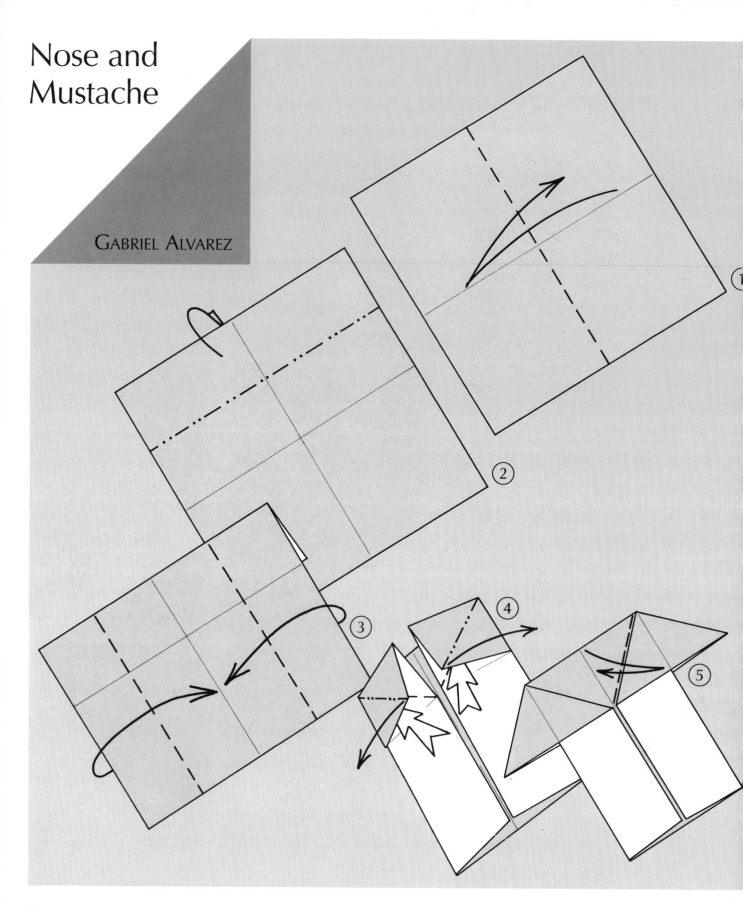

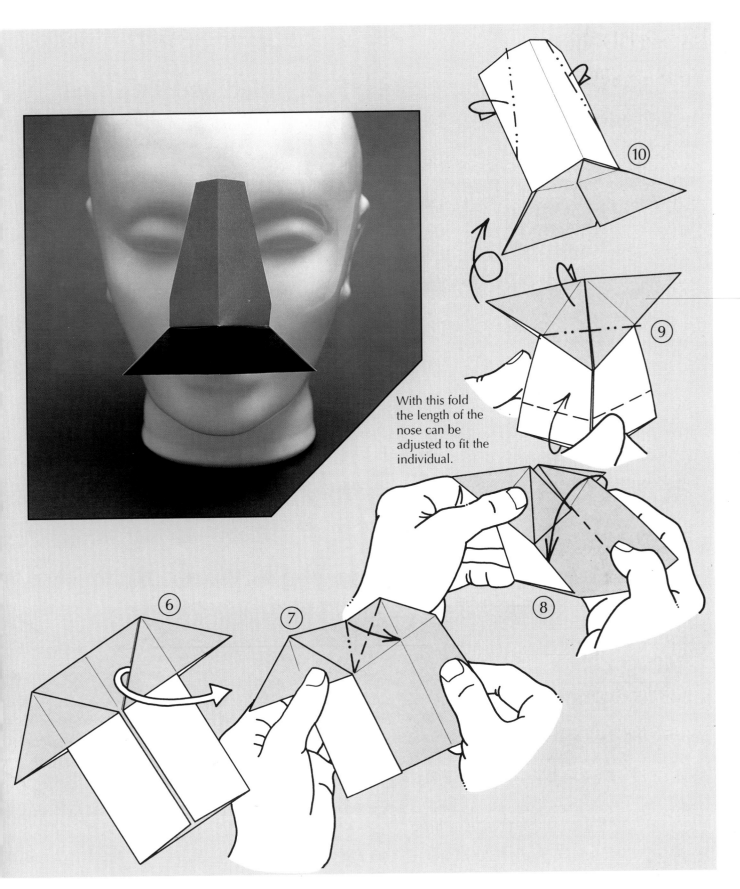

With this fold
the length of the
nose can be
adjusted to fit the
individual.

13

Paperholder

HUMI HUZITA

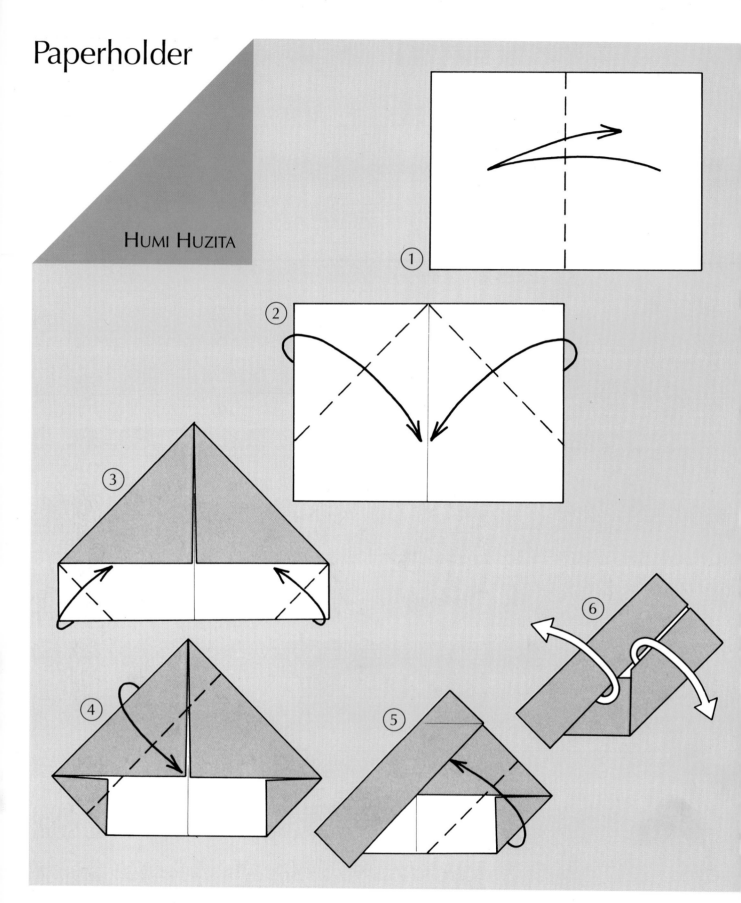

This model by Professor Humi Huzita can be used for many purposes. When paper size 11.6 x 8.25 in (29.7 x 21 cm) is used for this model, depending on the thickness of the paper, it will be suitable for a "caddy" with a base measuring approximately 4 x 4 in (10.5 x 10.5 cm) that can be used for holding memo-paper, and also for computer disks or for music cassettes. For the origami paperholder shown in the picture (base 6 x 6 in [15 x 15 cm]), I have used a starting size of 17 x 12 in (42.5 x 30.2 cm).

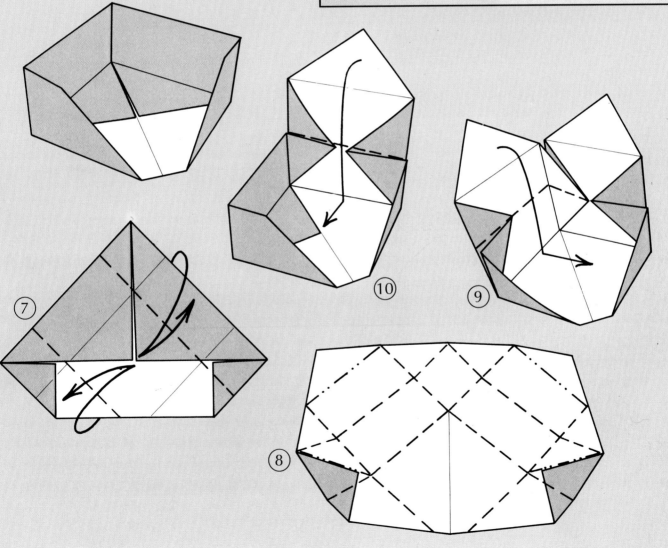

Double Hearts

FRANCIS OW

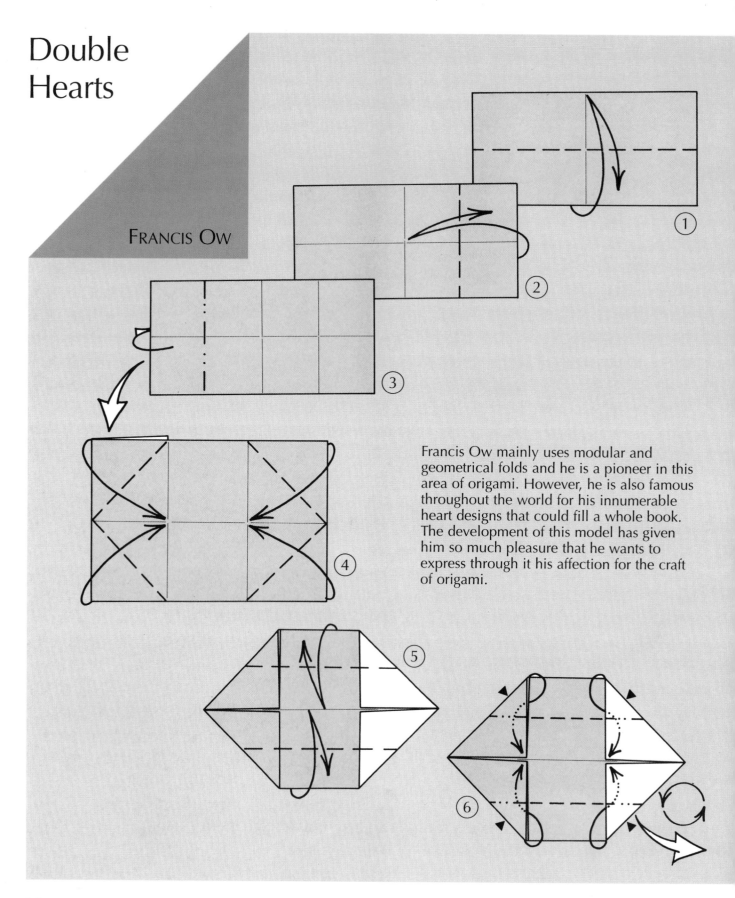

Francis Ow mainly uses modular and geometrical folds and he is a pioneer in this area of origami. However, he is also famous throughout the world for his innumerable heart designs that could fill a whole book. The development of this model has given him so much pleasure that he wants to express through it his affection for the craft of origami.

16

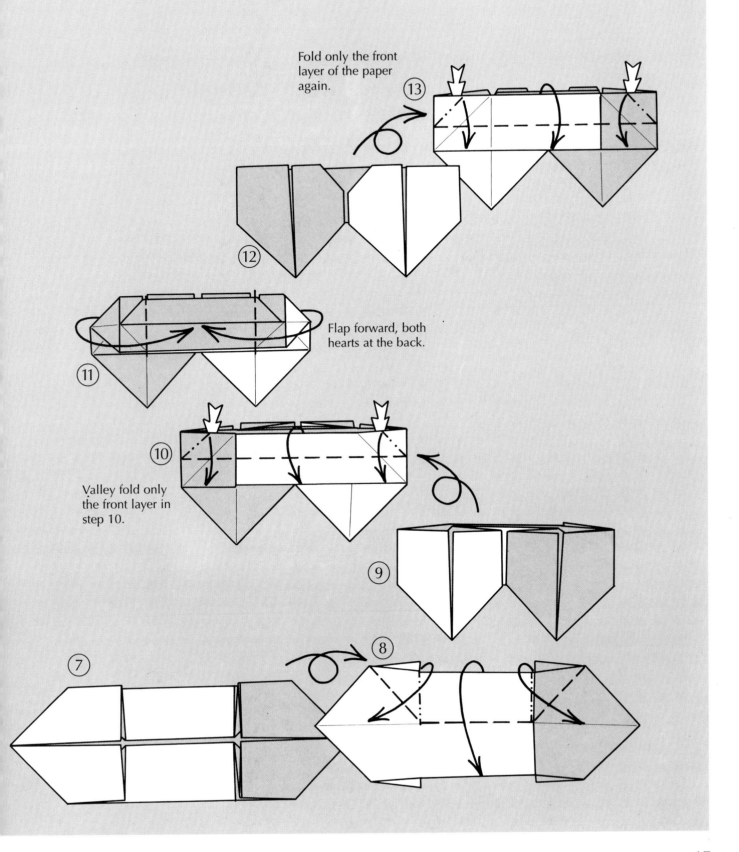

Fold only the front
layer of the paper
again.

⑬

⑫

Flap forward, both
hearts at the back.

⑪

⑩

Valley fold only
the front layer in
step 10.

⑨

⑦

⑧

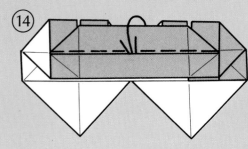

⑭

Hide the bridge
on the inside.

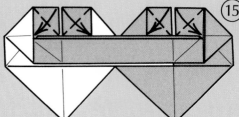

⑮

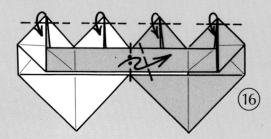

⑯

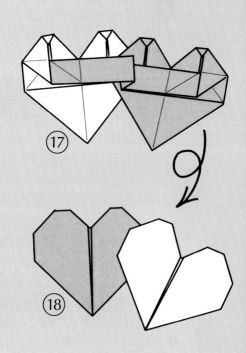

⑰

⑱

Cup

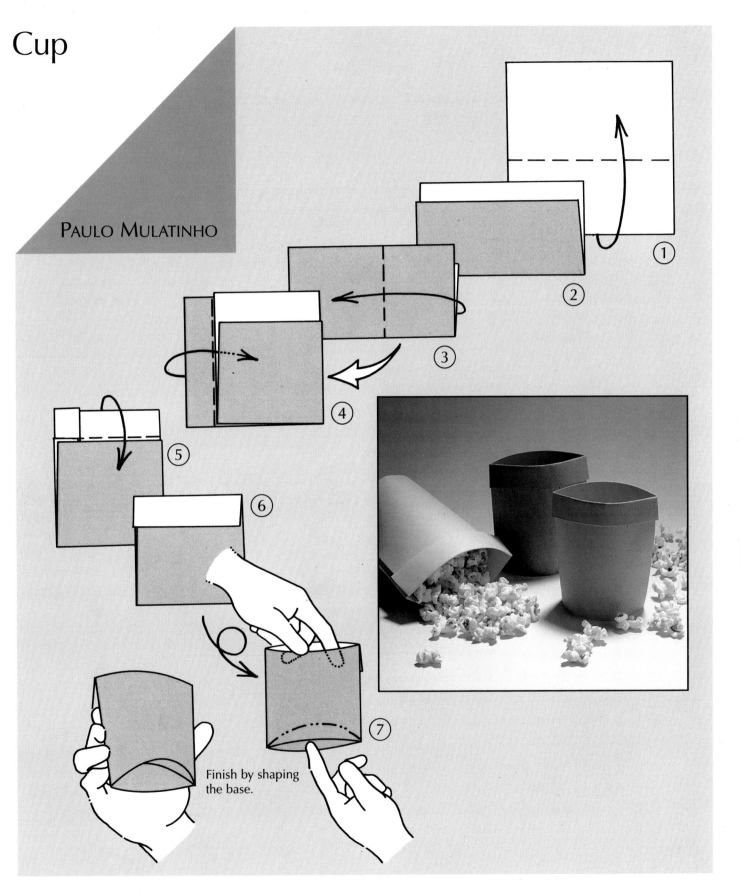

PAULO MULATINHO

① ② ③ ④ ⑤ ⑥ ⑦

Finish by shaping the base.

The Shirt Off One's Back

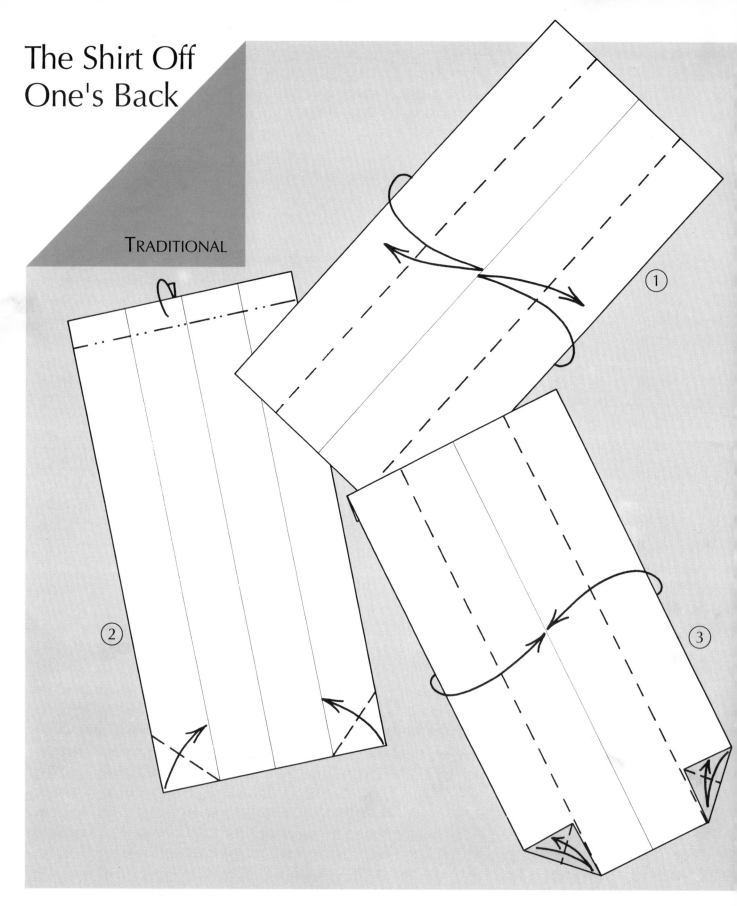

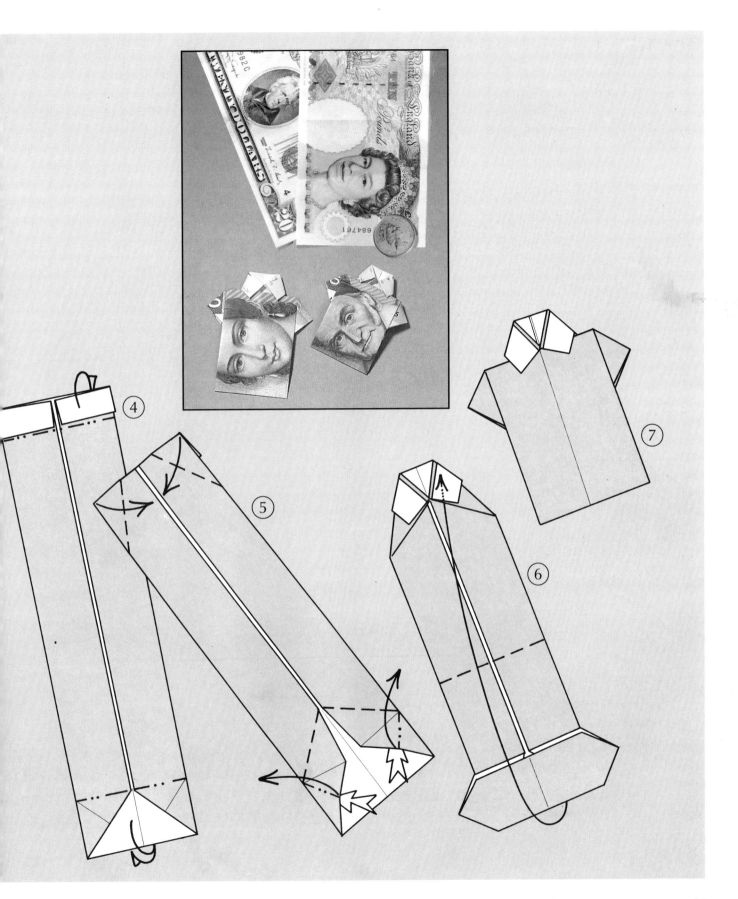

Arrow

PAULO MULATINHO

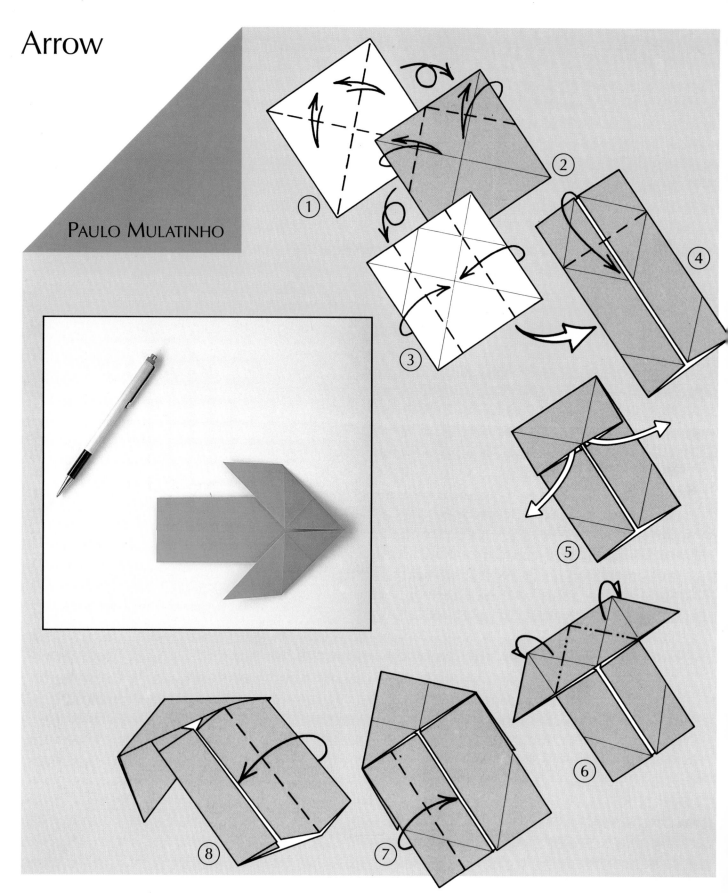

Object

THOKI YENN

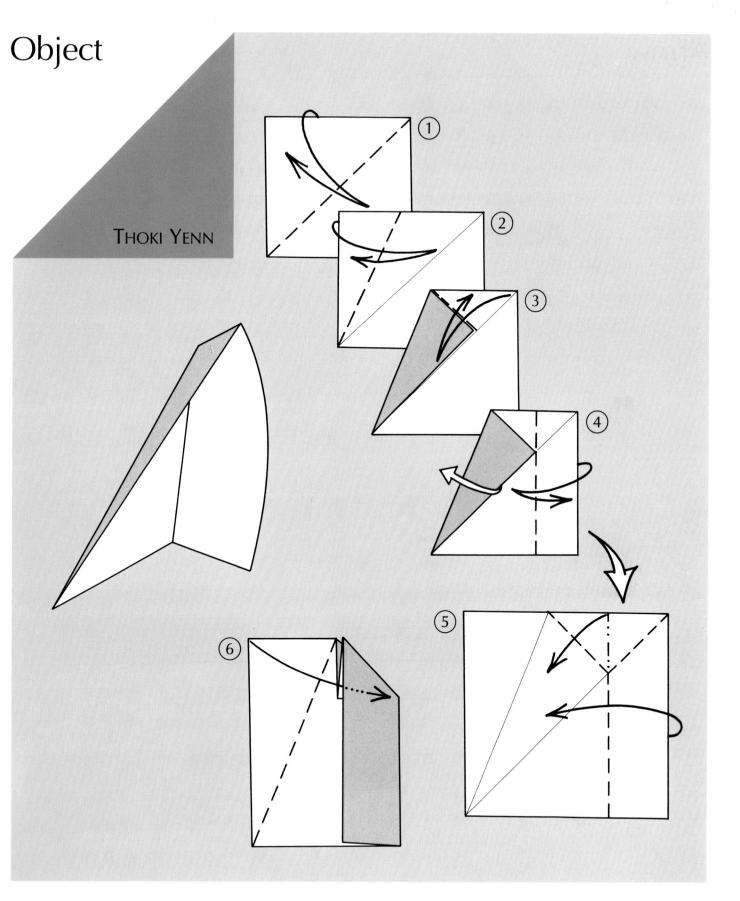

Nun

KUNIHIKO KASAHARA

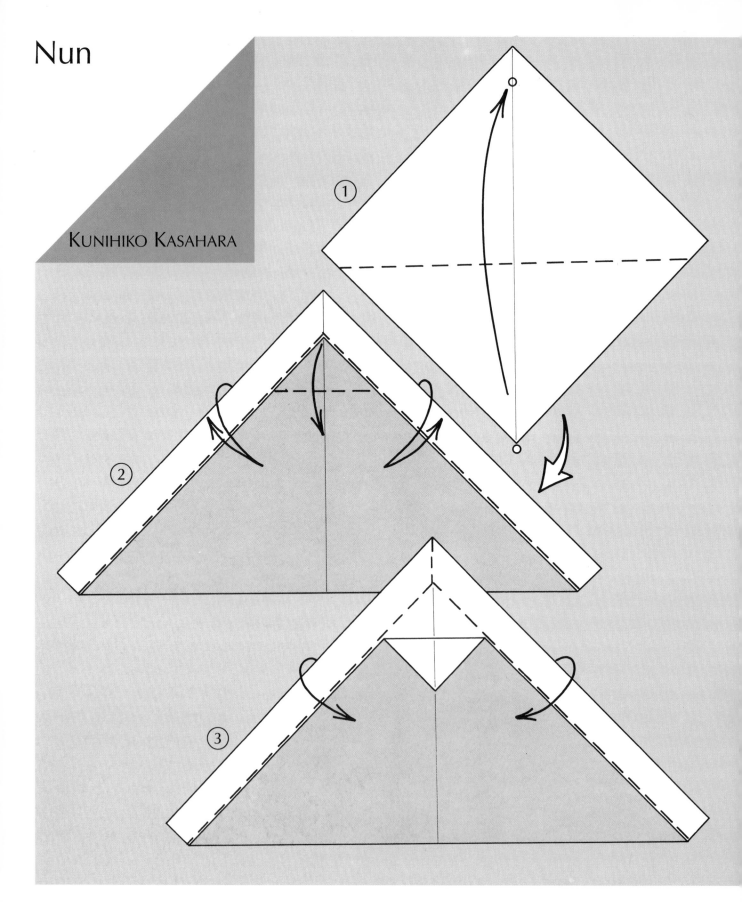

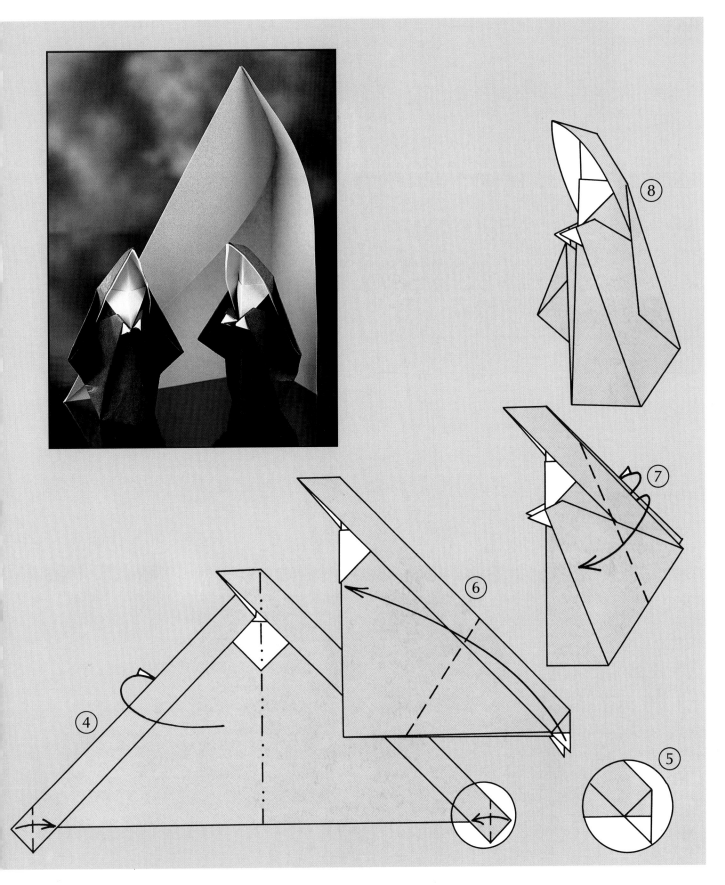

Pipe

EDWARD MEGRATH

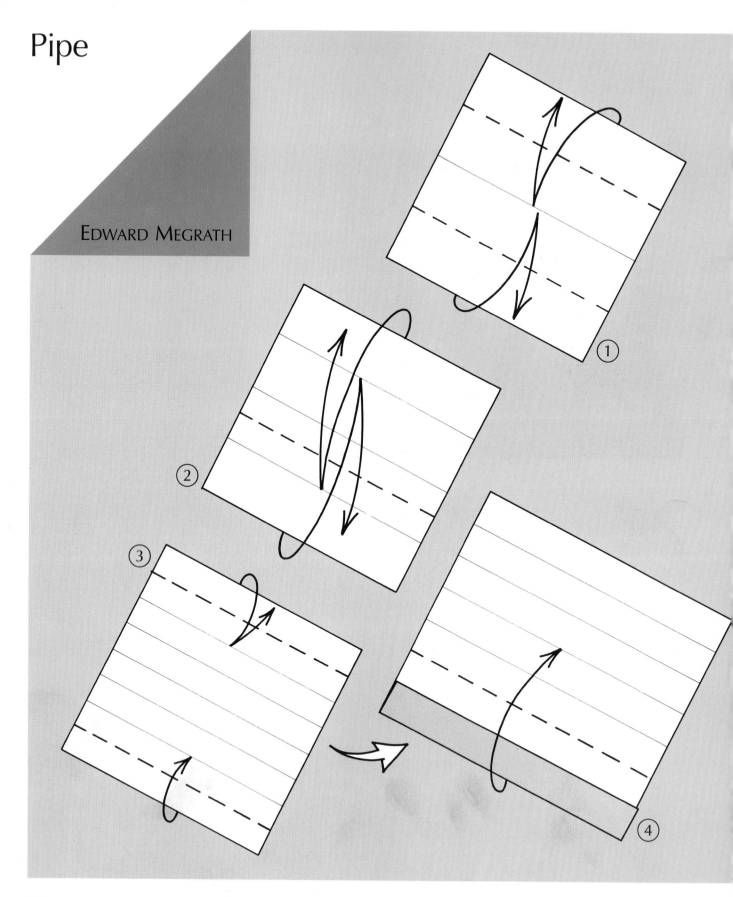

26

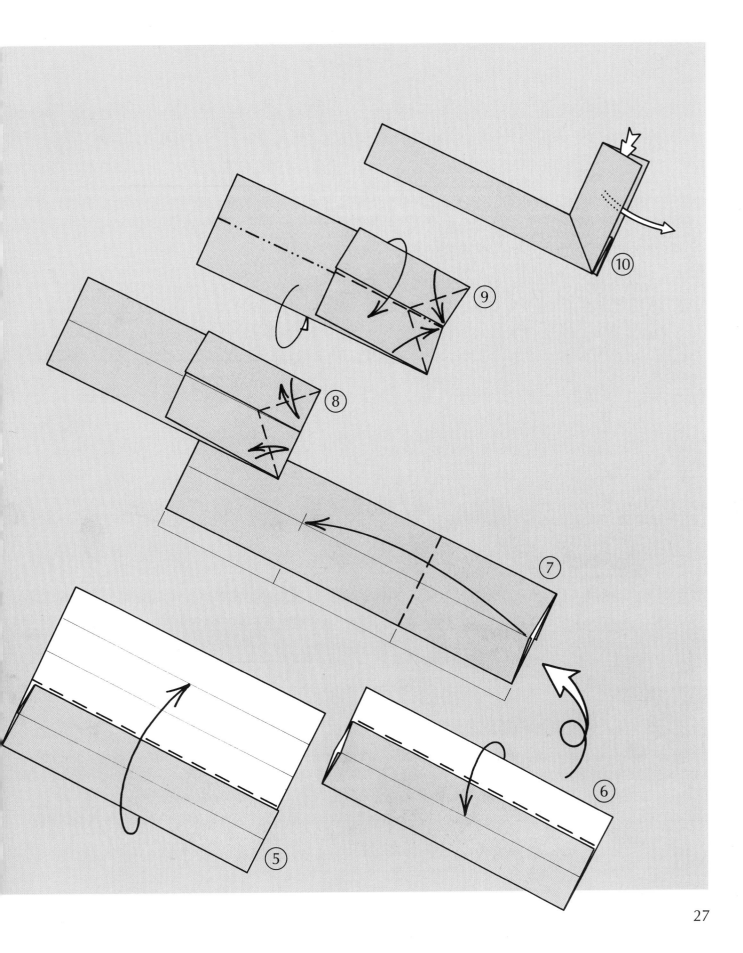

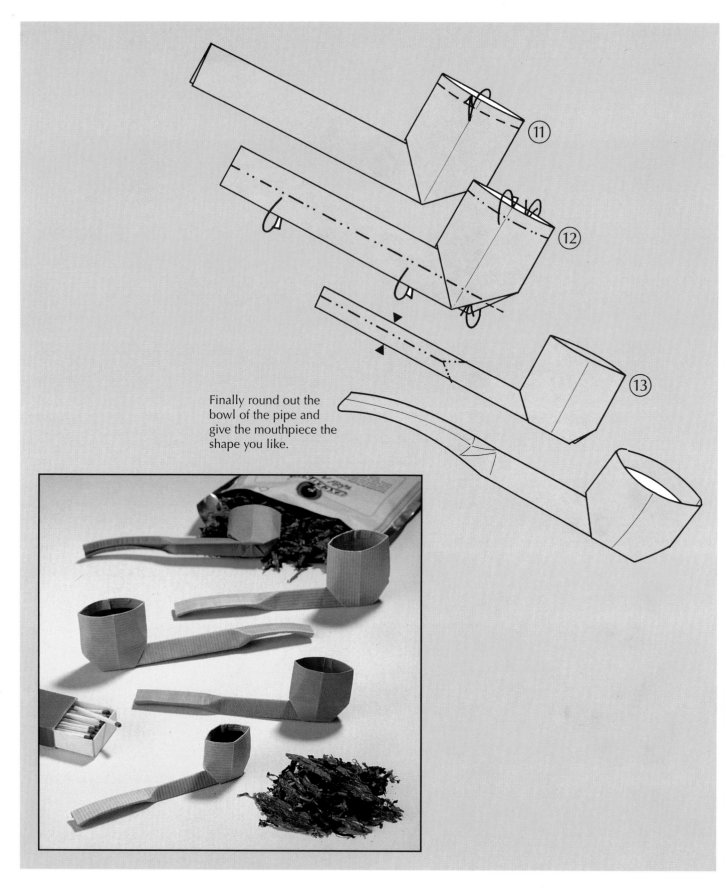

Finally round out the
bowl of the pipe and
give the mouthpiece the
shape you like.

⑪

⑫

⑬

Origami Zoo

Shy Young Hare

THOKI YENN

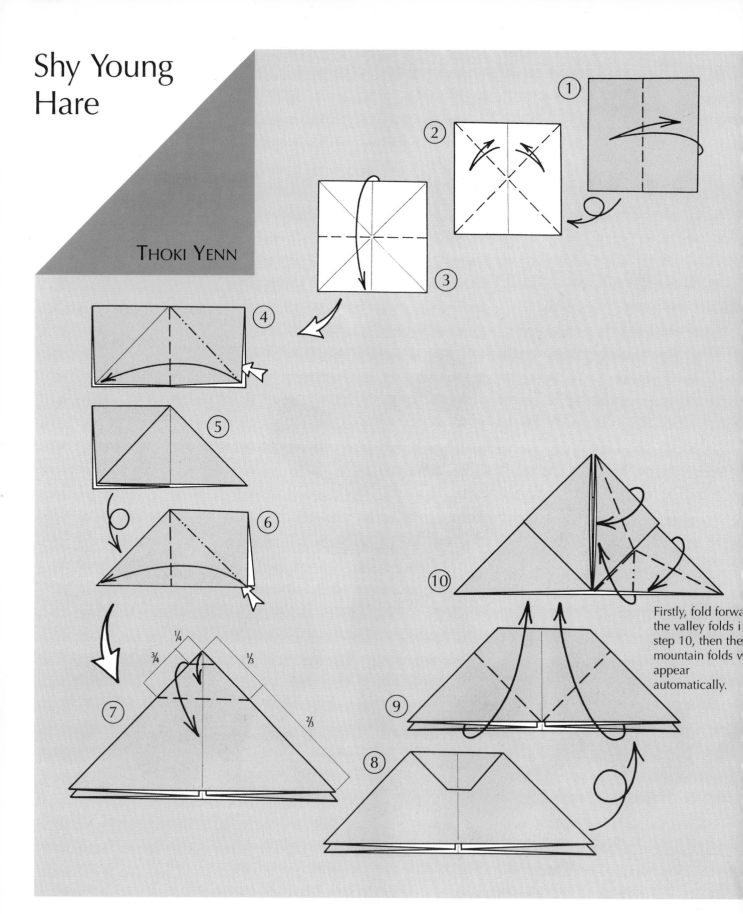

Firstly, fold forwa
the valley folds i
step 10, then the
mountain folds v
appear
automatically.

¼   ⅓
¾
⅔

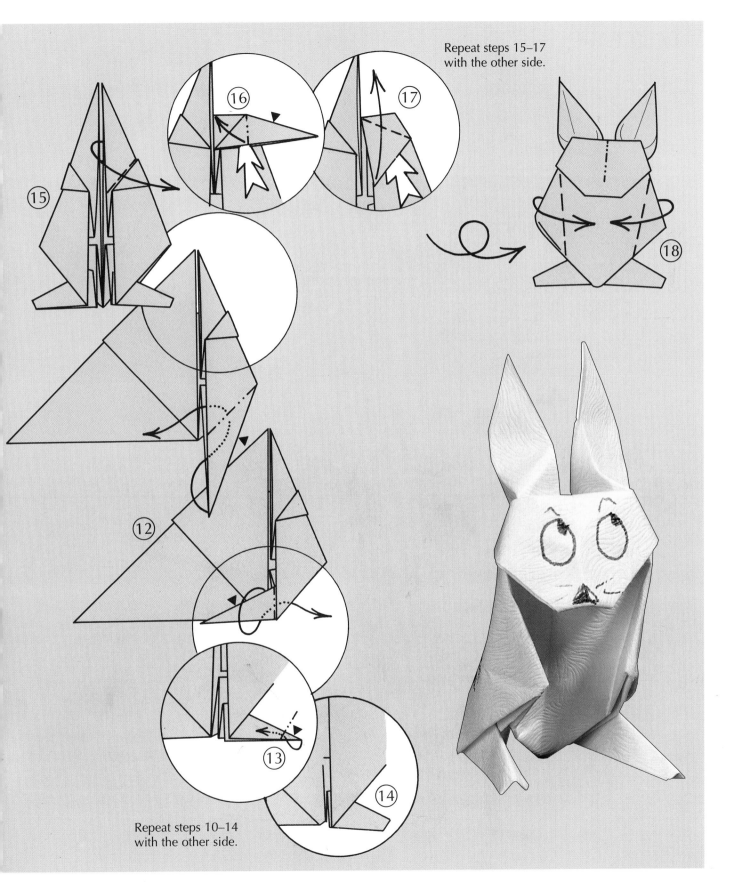

Repeat steps 15–17
with the other side.

Repeat steps 10–14
with the other side.

Elephant

EDWIN CORRIE

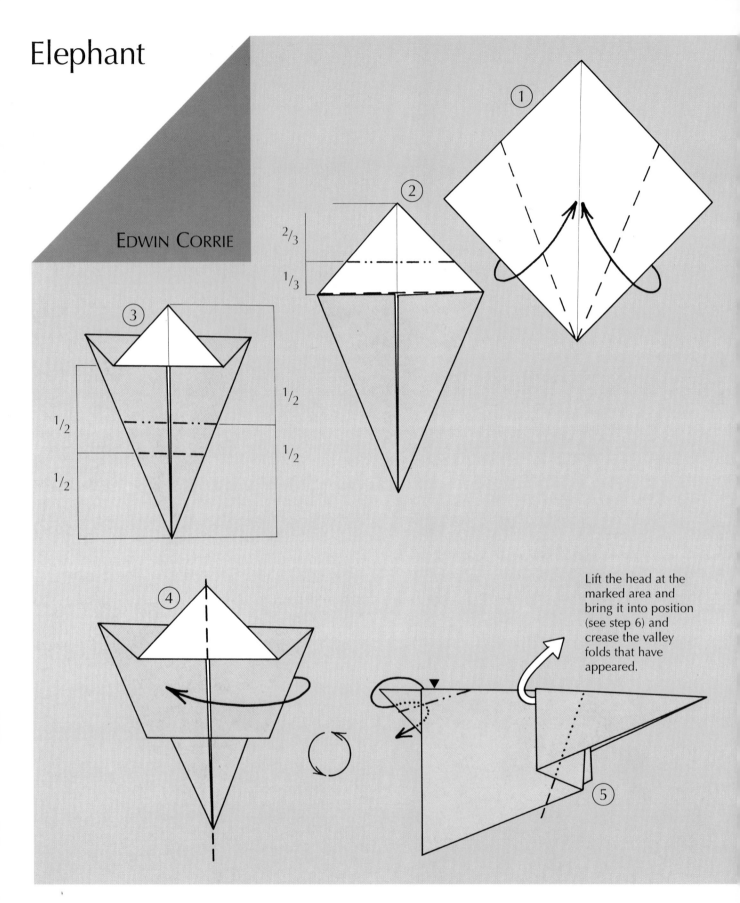

Lift the head at the marked area and bring it into position (see step 6) and crease the valley folds that have appeared.

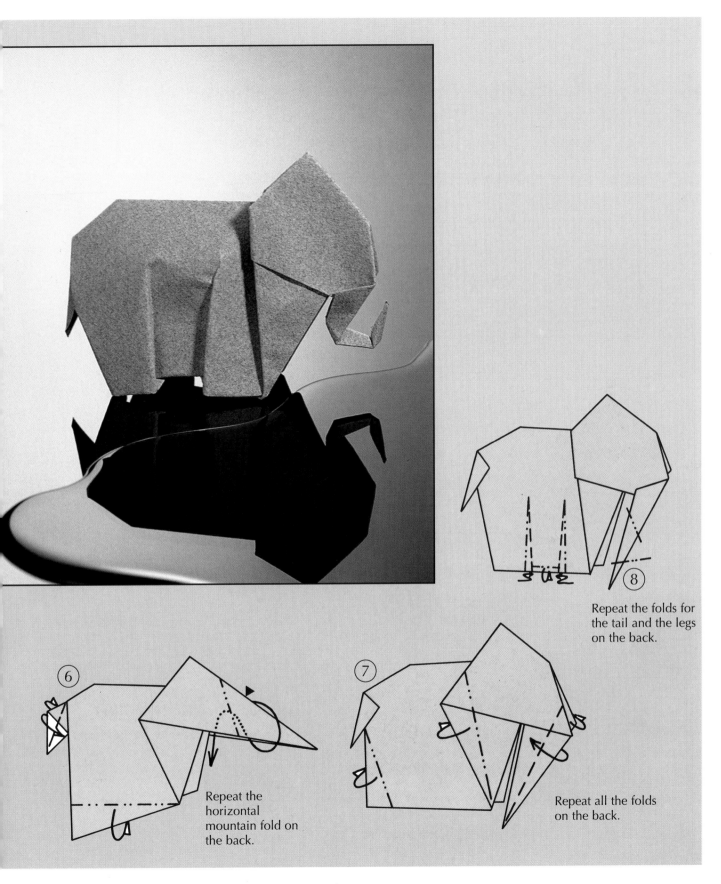

⑧

Repeat the folds for
the tail and the legs
on the back.

⑥

Repeat the
horizontal
mountain fold on
the back.

⑦

Repeat all the folds
on the back.

Frog

JUAN GIMENO

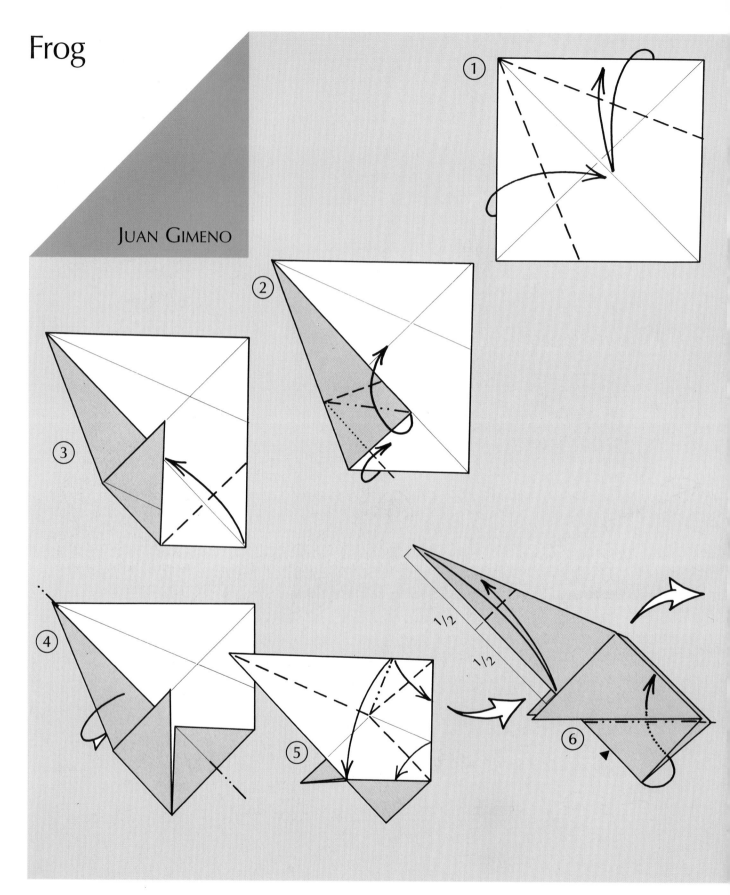

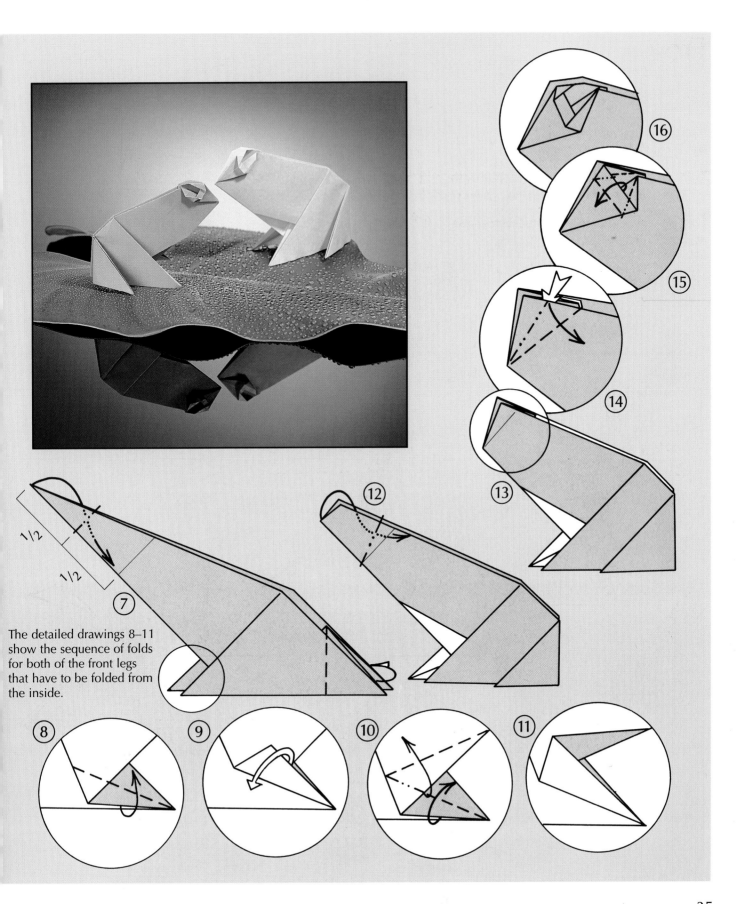

The detailed drawings 8–11 show the sequence of folds for both of the front legs that have to be folded from the inside.

Mouse

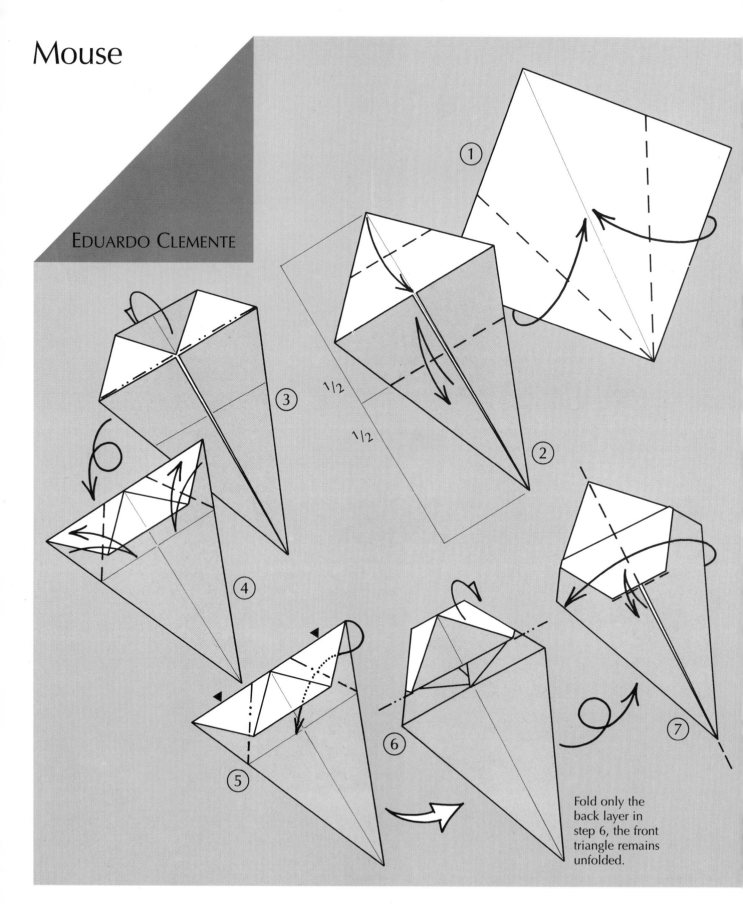

EDUARDO CLEMENTE

① ② ③ ④ ⑤ ⑥ ⑦

1/2
1/2

Fold only the back layer in step 6, the front triangle remains unfolded.

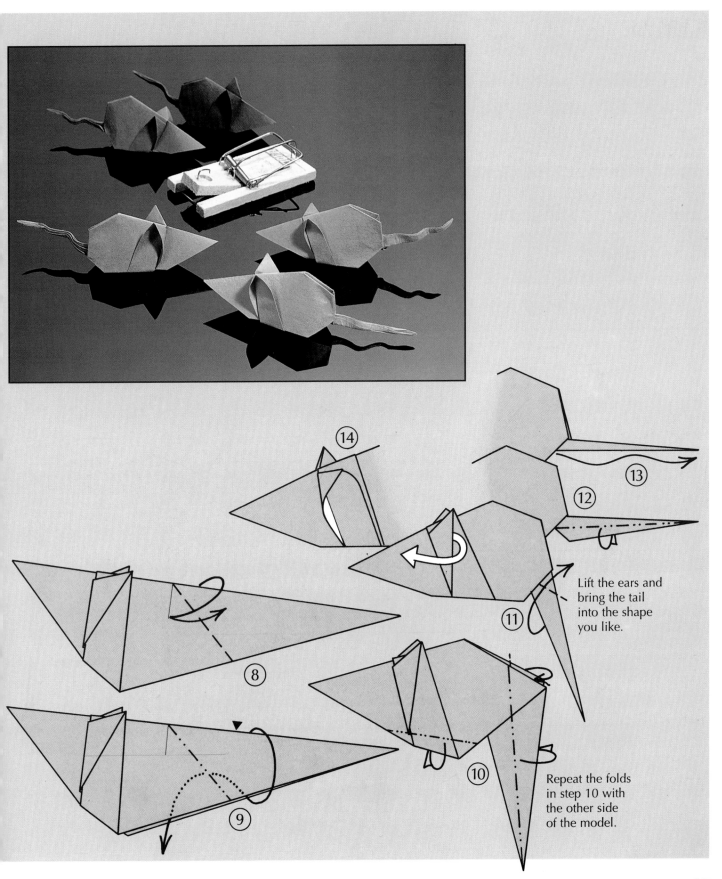

⑭

⑬

⑫

⑪

Lift the ears and
bring the tail
into the shape
you like.

⑧

⑨

⑩

Repeat the folds
in step 10 with
the other side
of the model.

Panda

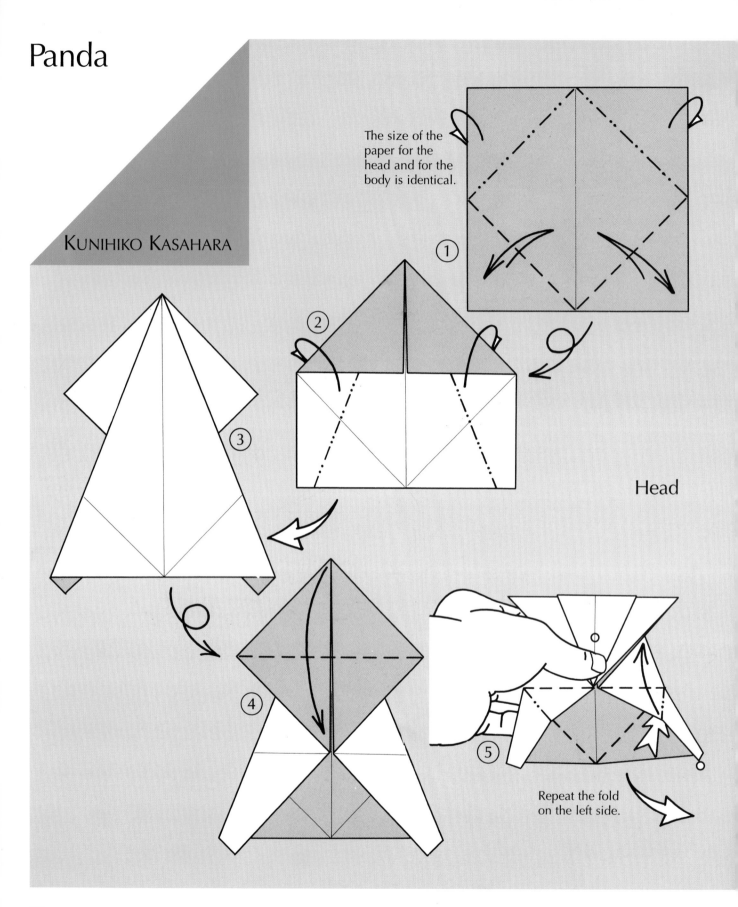

KUNIHIKO KASAHARA

The size of the paper for the head and for the body is identical.

① ② ③ ④ ⑤

Head

Repeat the fold on the left side.

38

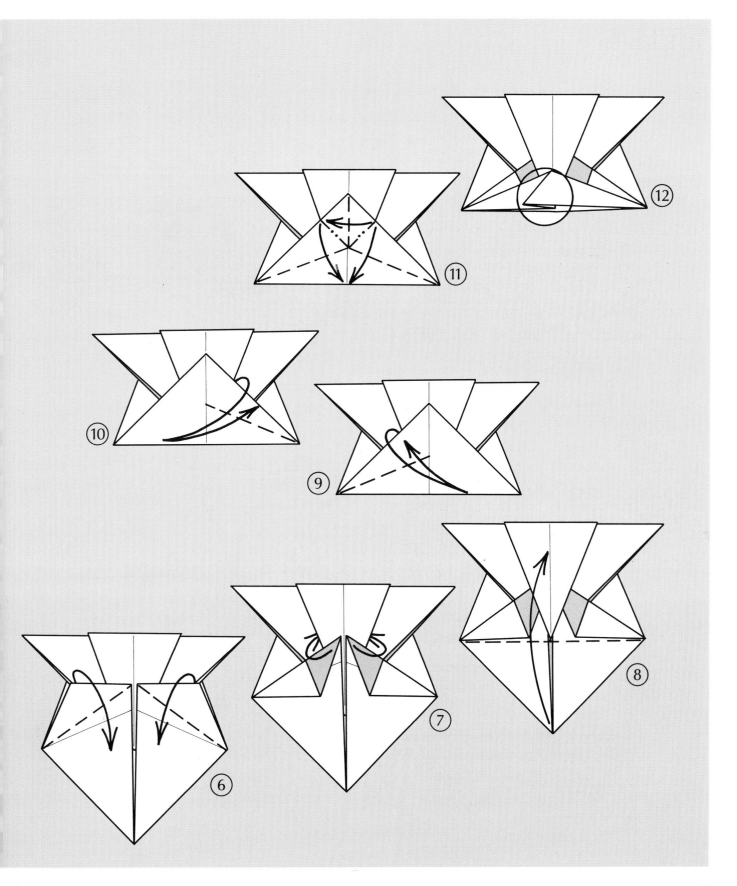

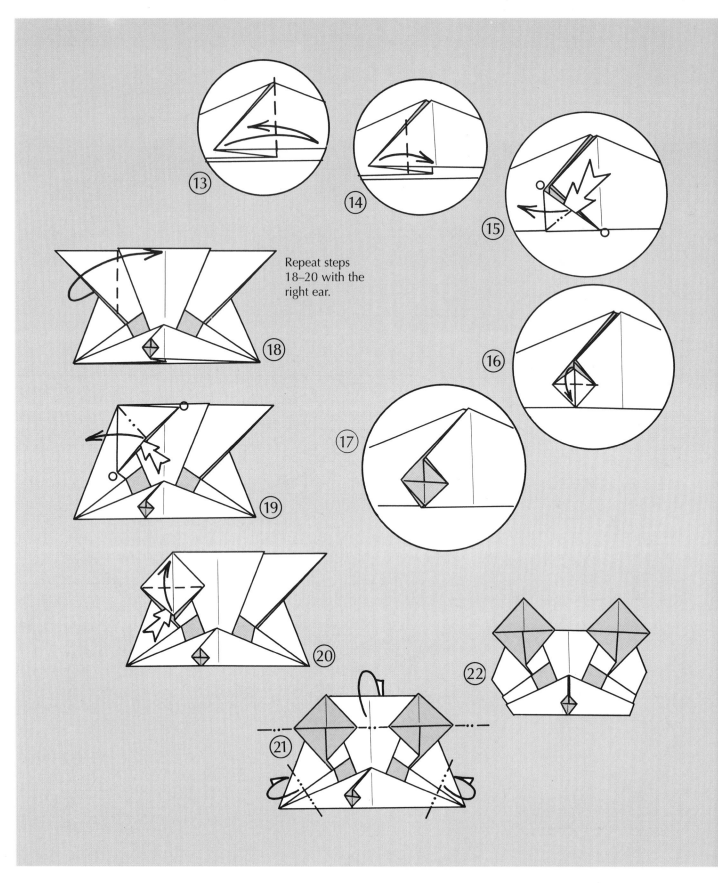

Repeat steps
18–20 with the
right ear.

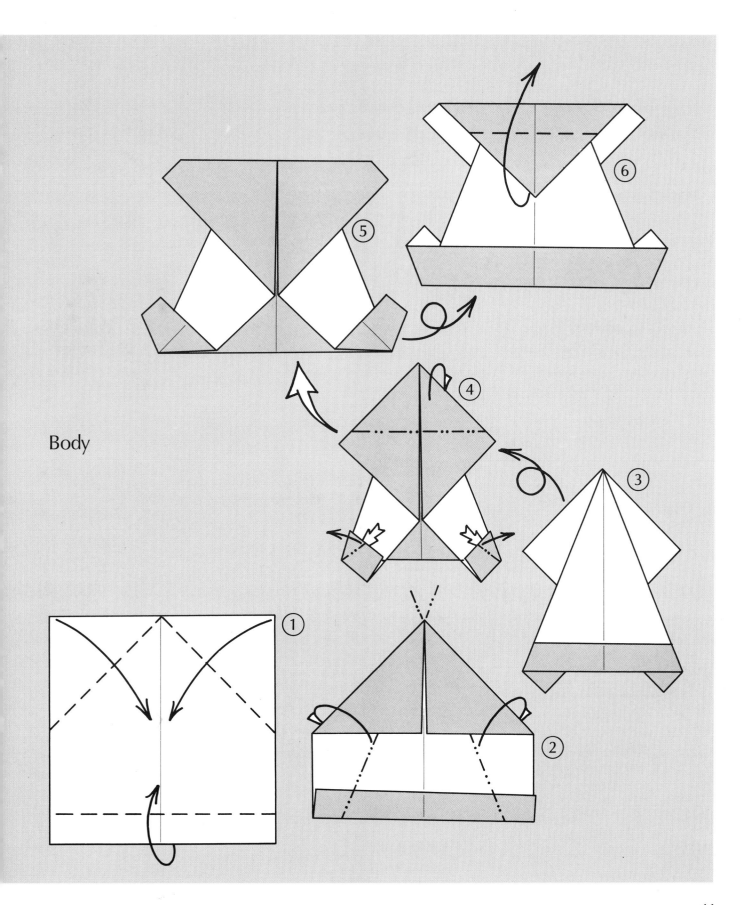

Body

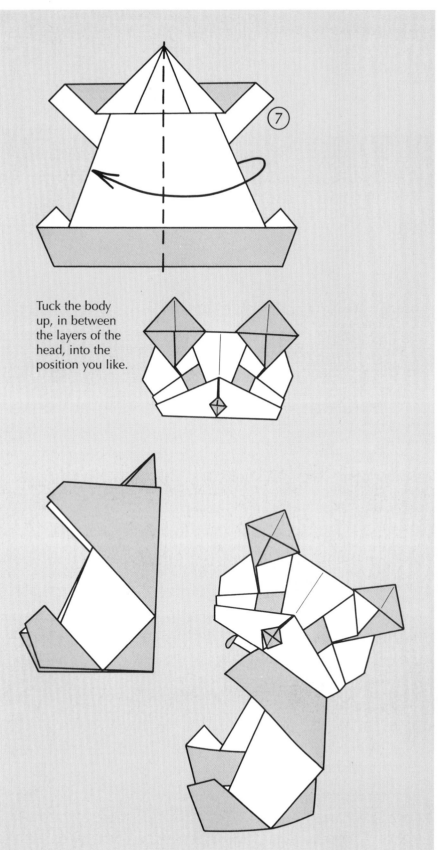

⑦

Tuck the body up, in between the layers of the head, into the position you like.

For a
Desk Top

Picture
Frame

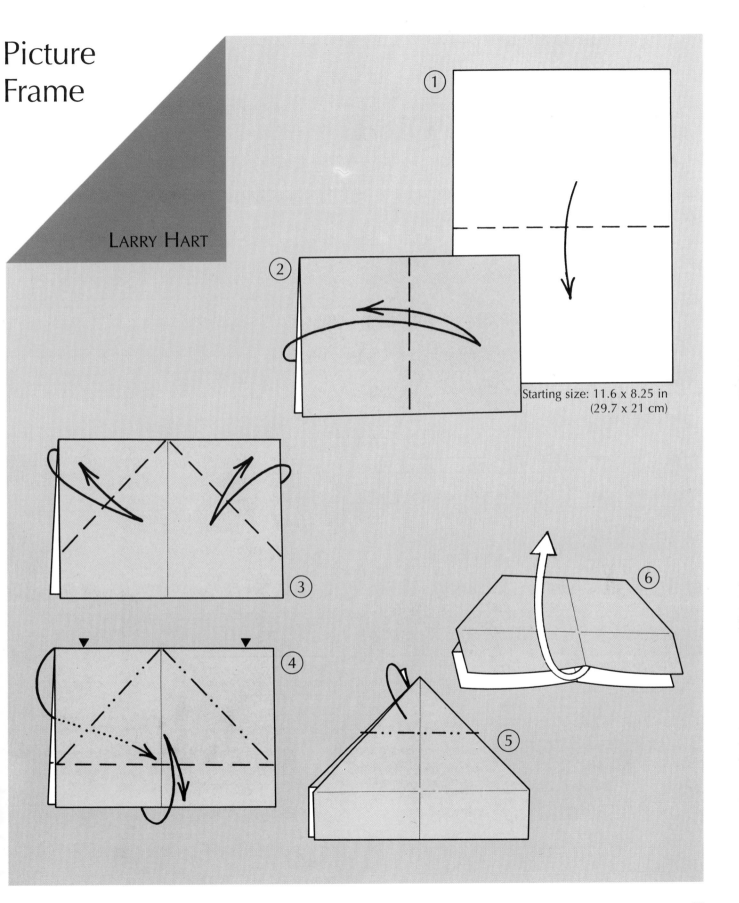

LARRY HART

Starting size: 11.6 x 8.25 in
(29.7 x 21 cm)

In steps 9 and 10 fold the horizontal and vertical edges to correspond with the size of the picture to be framed. The example shown here is a postcard, size 4 x 6 in (10.5 x 15 cm).

Take out the picture after you have folded the creases in step 10.

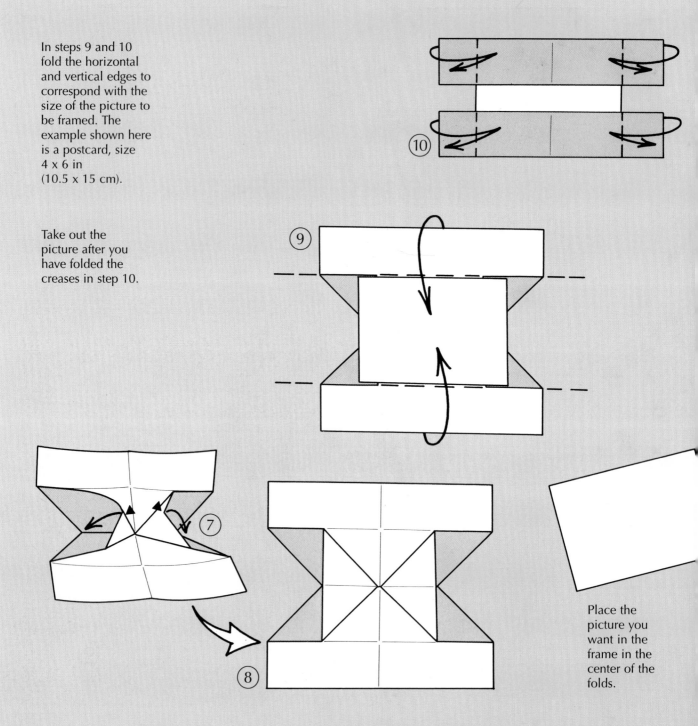

10

9

7

8

Place the picture you want in the frame in the center of the folds.

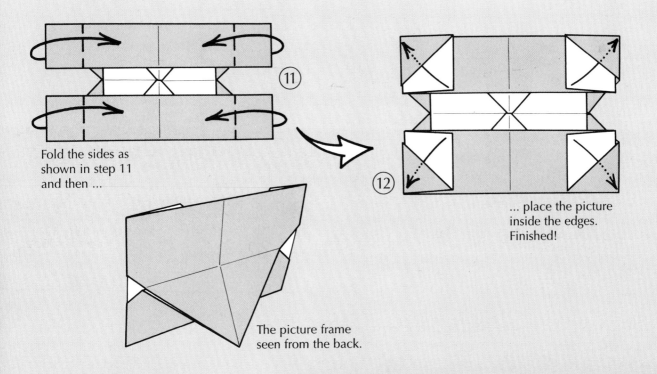

⑪

Fold the sides as
shown in step 11
and then ...

⑫

... place the picture
inside the edges.
Finished!

The picture frame
seen from the back.

Note Book

MARTIN WALL

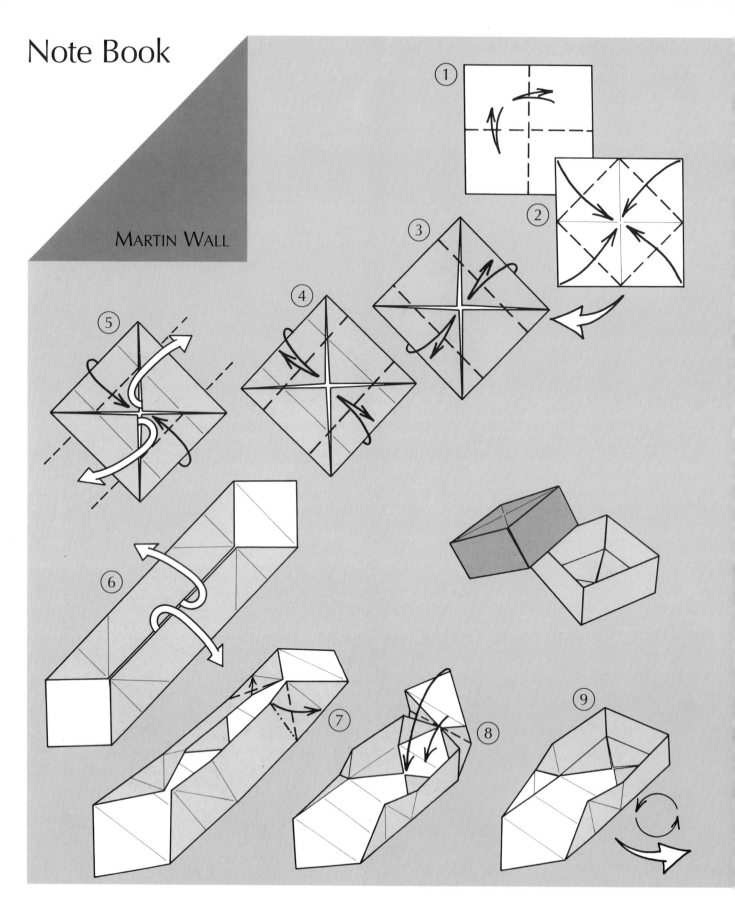

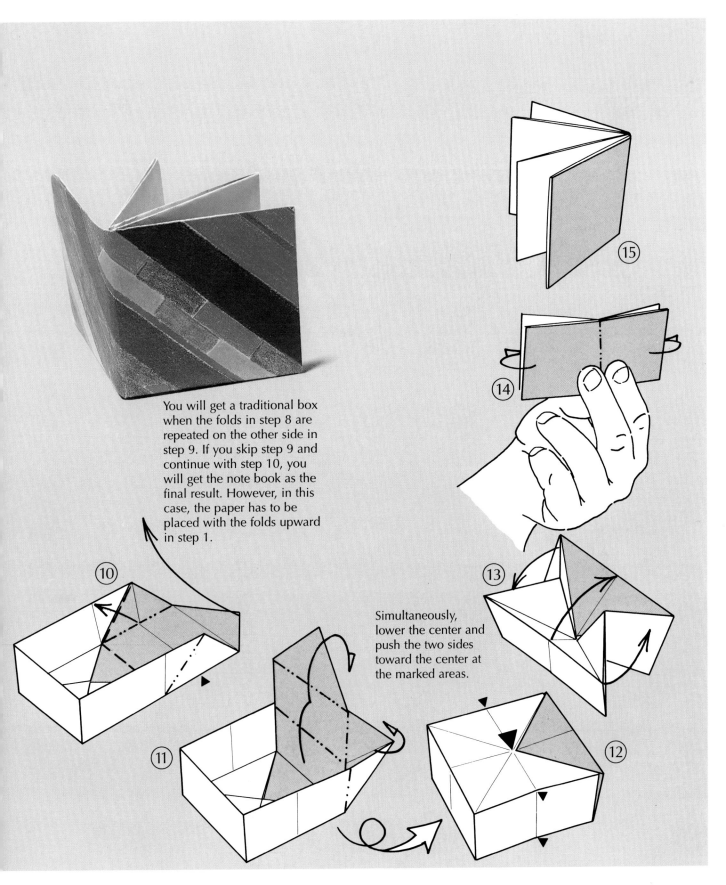

You will get a traditional box when the folds in step 8 are repeated on the other side in step 9. If you skip step 9 and continue with step 10, you will get the note book as the final result. However, in this case, the paper has to be placed with the folds upward in step 1.

Simultaneously, lower the center and push the two sides toward the center at the marked areas.

49

Container

GIUSEPPE BAGGI

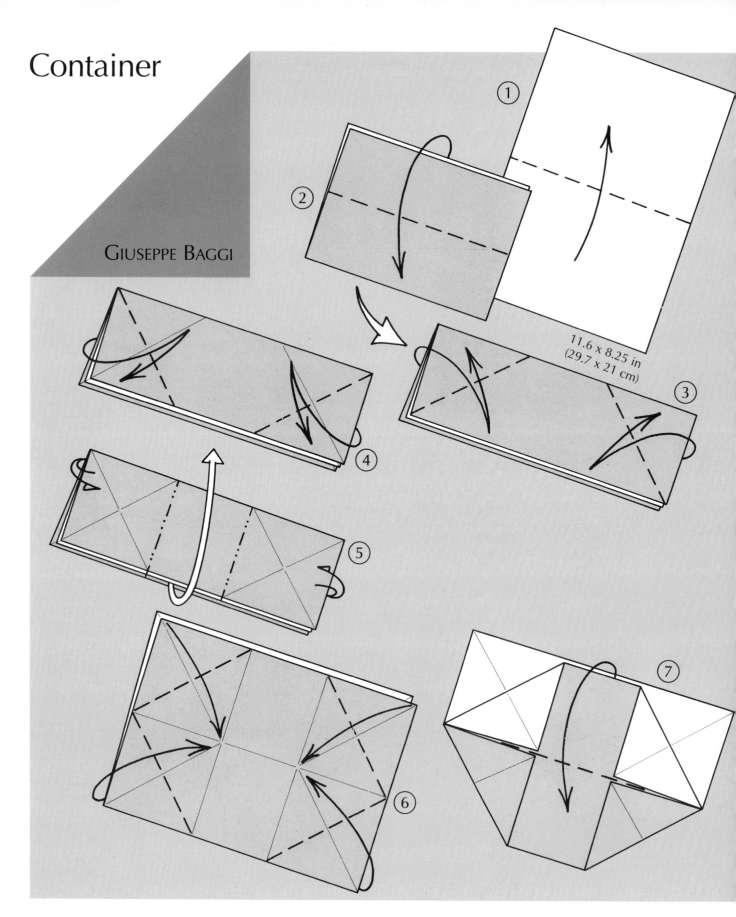

11.6 x 8.25 in
(29.7 x 21 cm)

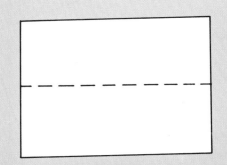

This container is the final result when the paper is not divided diagonally but lengthways in step 1 and the remainder of the steps are carried out with the new starting base.

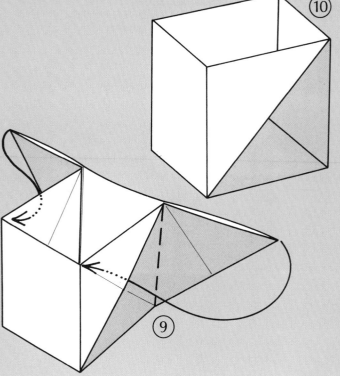

⑩

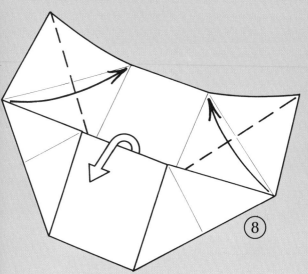

⑧

⑨

Folder

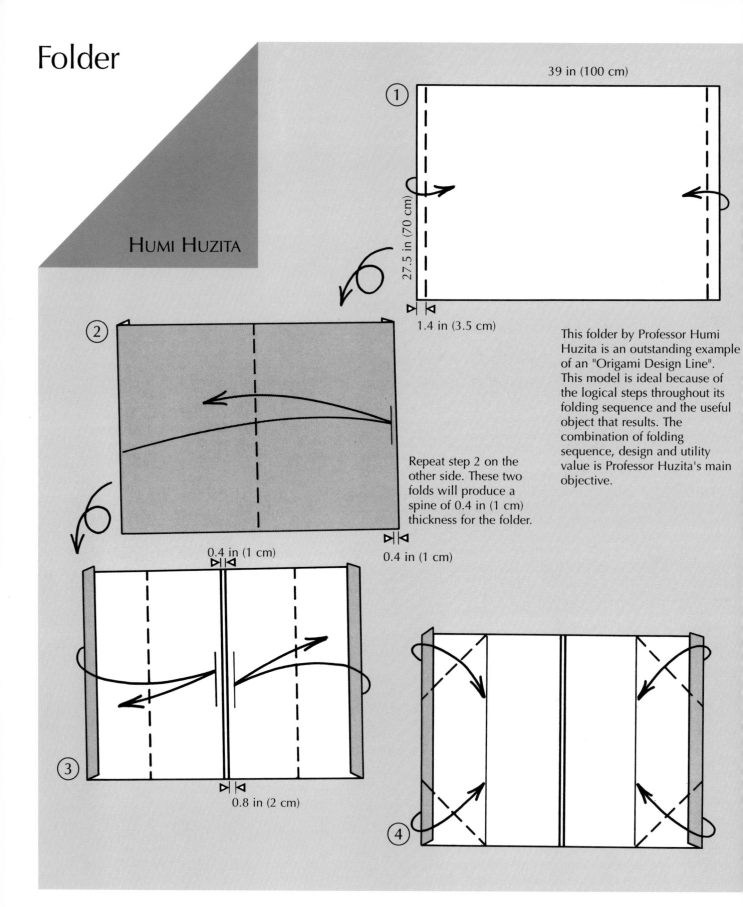

HUMI HUZITA

39 in (100 cm)

① 27.5 in (70 cm)

1.4 in (3.5 cm)

This folder by Professor Humi Huzita is an outstanding example of an "Origami Design Line". This model is ideal because of the logical steps throughout its folding sequence and the useful object that results. The combination of folding sequence, design and utility value is Professor Huzita's main objective.

② Repeat step 2 on the other side. These two folds will produce a spine of 0.4 in (1 cm) thickness for the folder.

0.4 in (1 cm)

0.4 in (1 cm)

③ 0.4 in (1 cm)

0.8 in (2 cm)

④

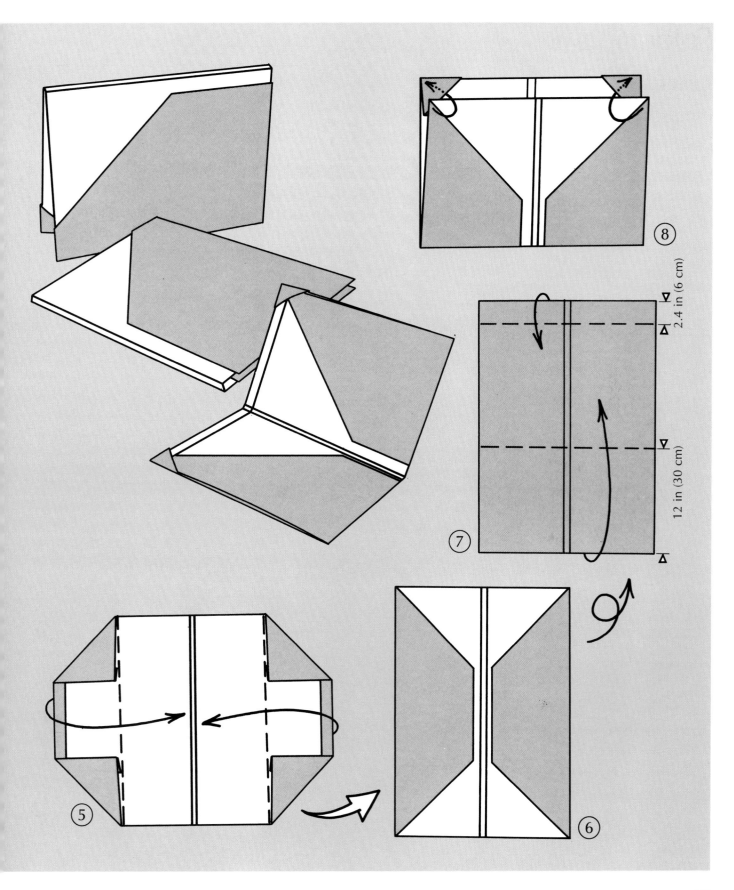

⑧

2.4 in (6 cm)

12 in (30 cm)

⑦

⑤

⑥

Daisy's
Envelope

NICK ROBINSON

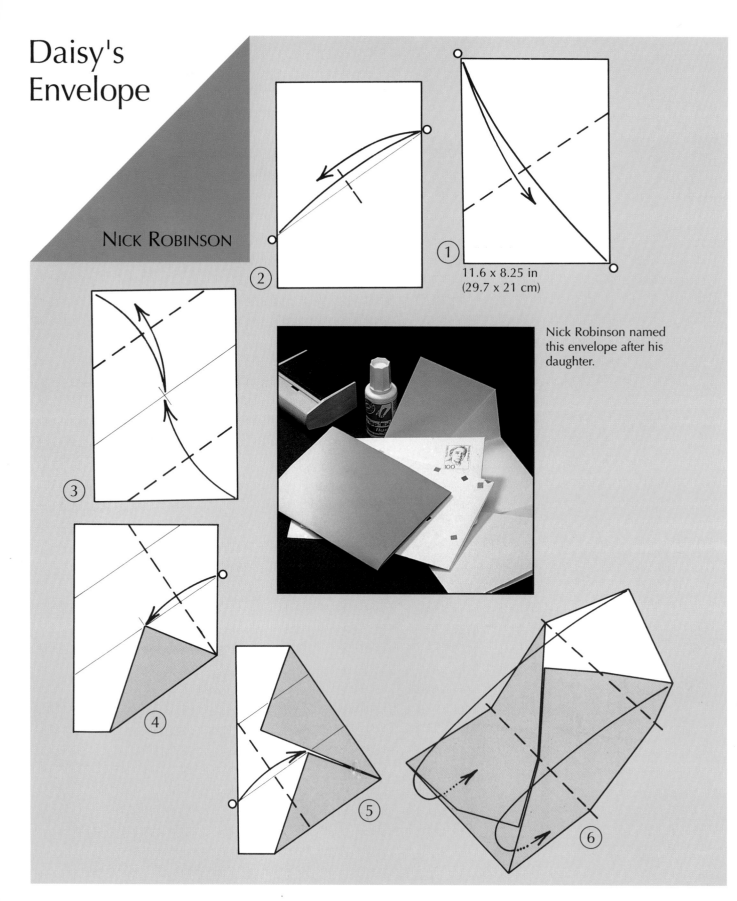

① 11.6 x 8.25 in
(29.7 x 21 cm)

Nick Robinson named
this envelope after his
daughter.

54

Presenting
Gifts

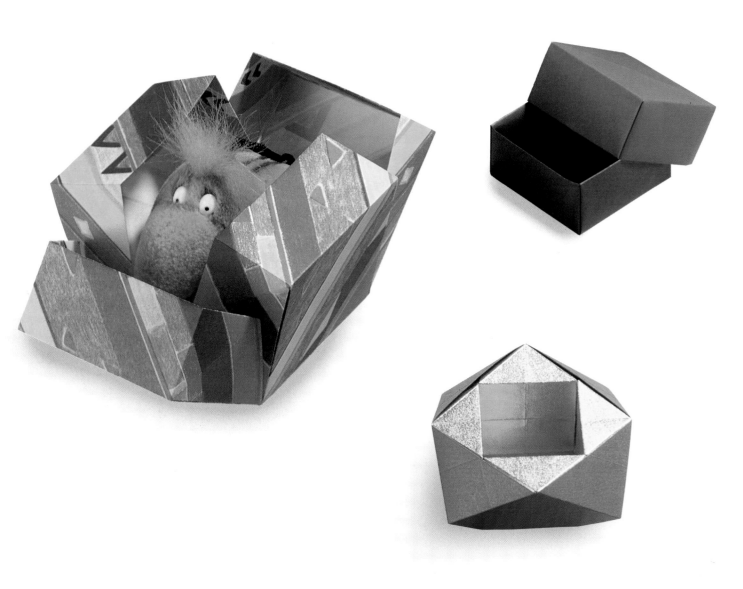

Bowl

PHILIP SHEN
attributed to

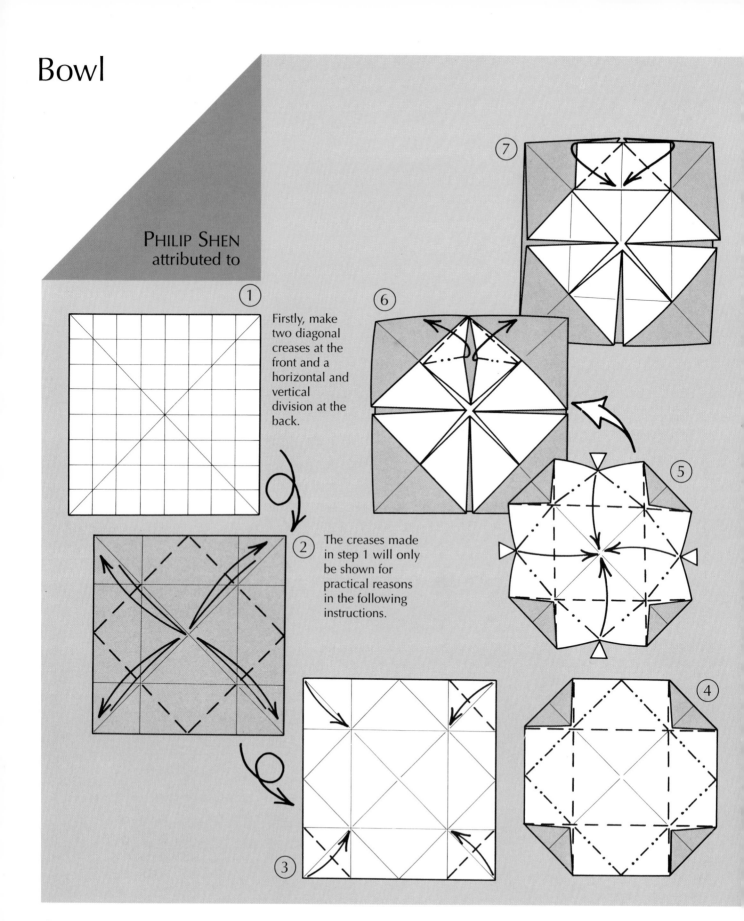

① Firstly, make two diagonal creases at the front and a horizontal and vertical division at the back.

② The creases made in step 1 will only be shown for practical reasons in the following instructions.

56

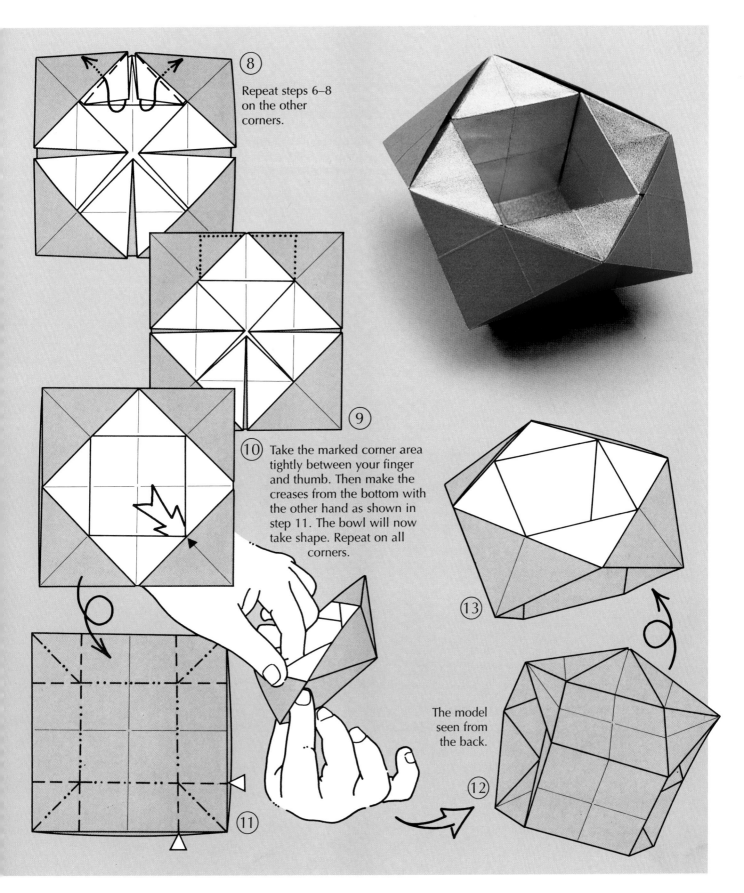

⑧ Repeat steps 6–8 on the other corners.

⑨

⑩ Take the marked corner area tightly between your finger and thumb. Then make the creases from the bottom with the other hand as shown in step 11. The bowl will now take shape. Repeat on all corners.

⑪

⑬

The model seen from the back.

⑫

Gift
Box

GIOVANNI
MALTAGLIATTI

Paper size: you need a
relatively large square for
the gift box. For instance, if
the completed box should
have an edge of 2.4 in
(6 cm), the paper size
needs to be 9.8 x 9.8 in
(25 x 25 cm).

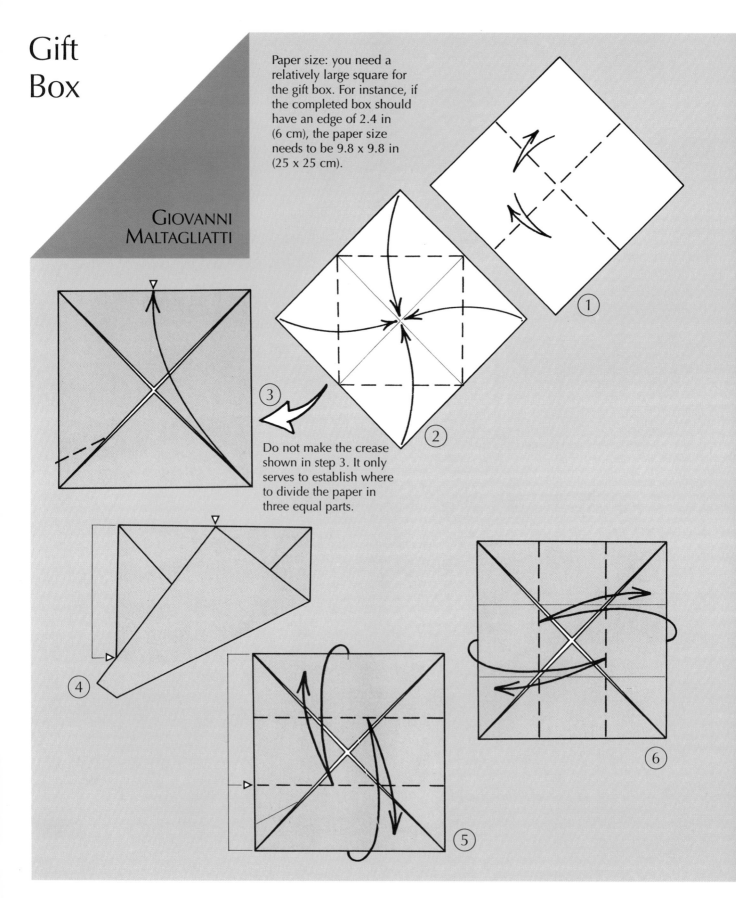

Do not make the crease
shown in step 3. It only
serves to establish where
to divide the paper in
three equal parts.

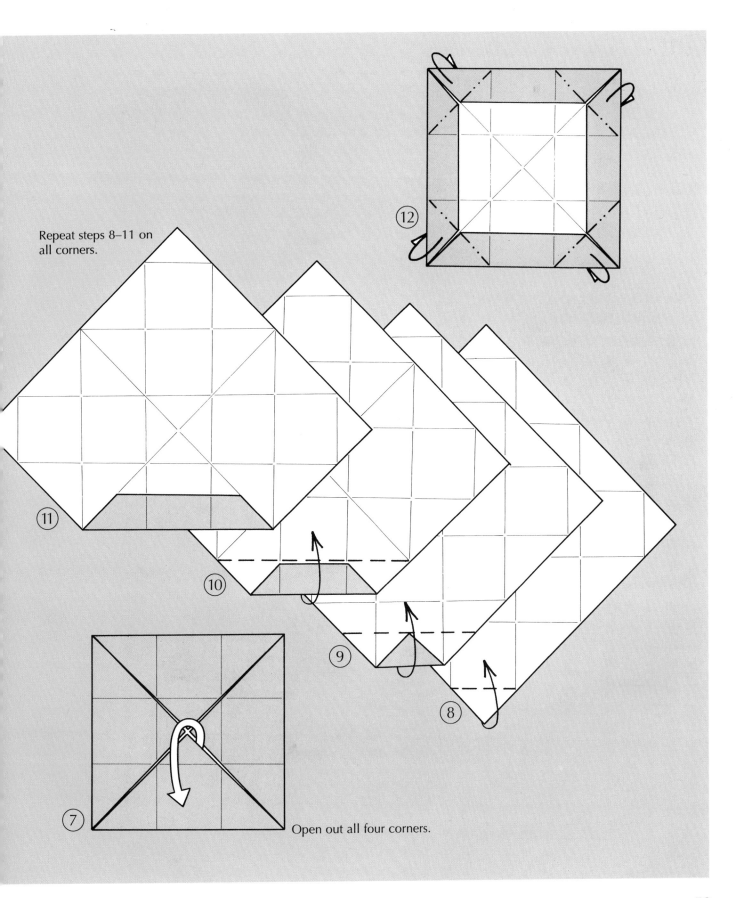

Repeat steps 8–11 on all corners.

Open out all four corners.

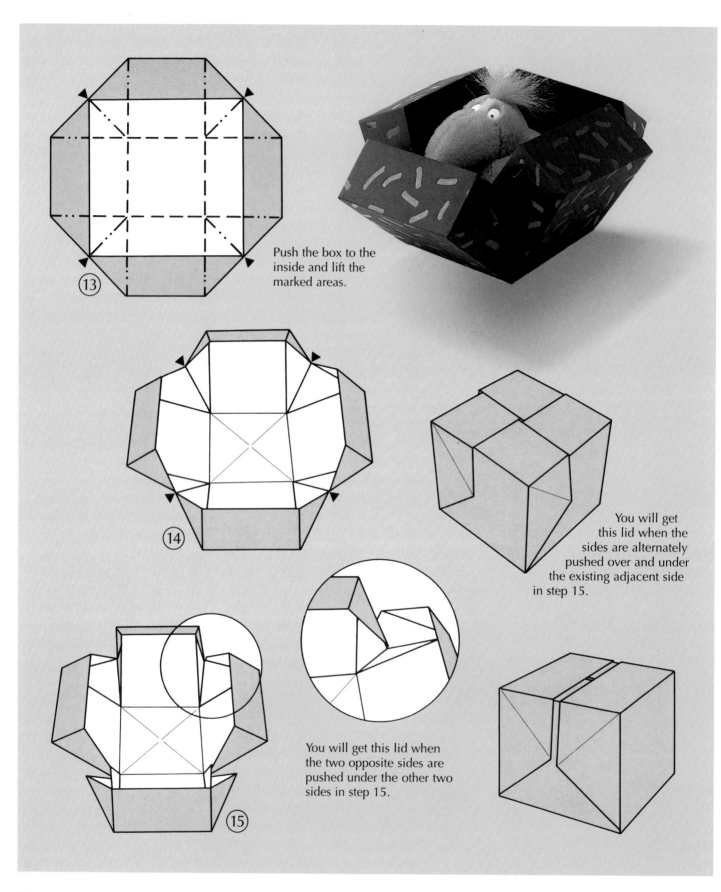

Push the box to the
inside and lift the
marked areas.

⑬

⑭

You will get
this lid when the
sides are alternately
pushed over and under
the existing adjacent side
in step 15.

You will get this lid when
the two opposite sides are
pushed under the other two
sides in step 15.

⑮

Christmas
Decorations

Star

PAOLO BASCETTA

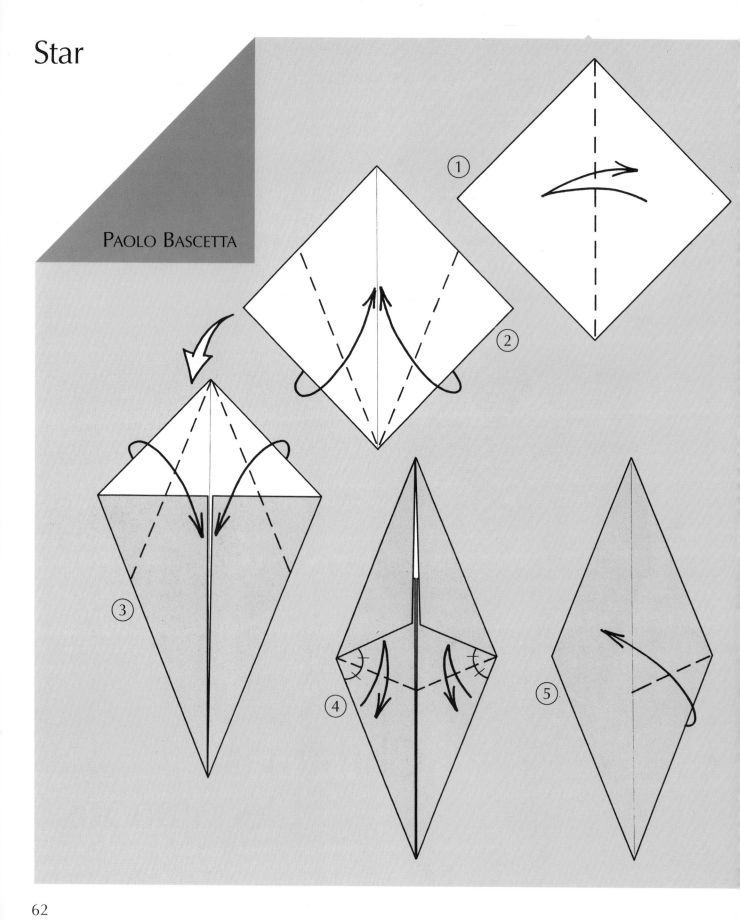

62

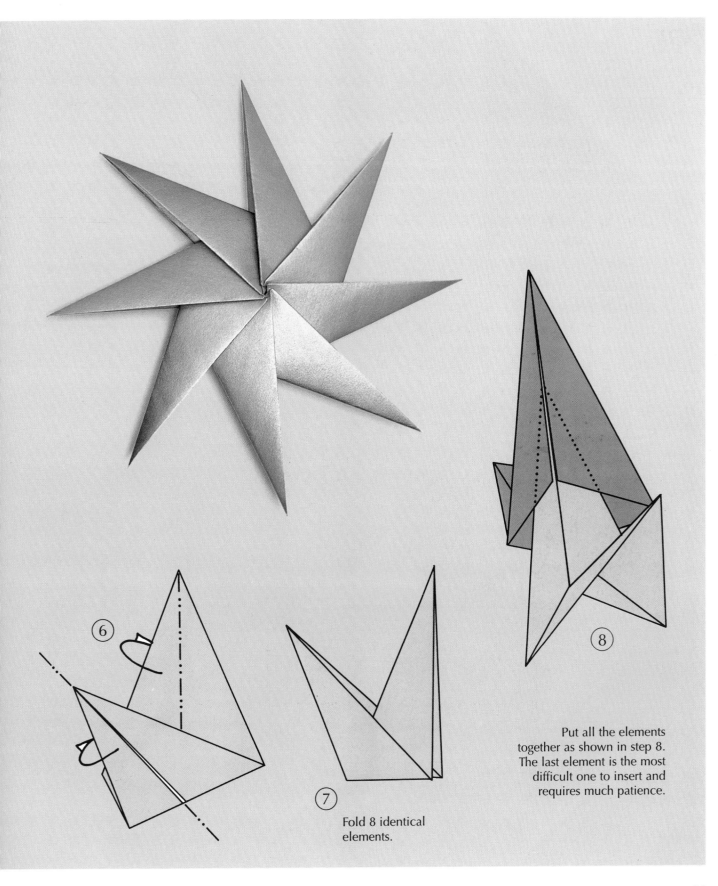

⑥

⑦ Fold 8 identical elements.

⑧

Put all the elements together as shown in step 8. The last element is the most difficult one to insert and requires much patience.

63

Angel

ALFREDO GIUNTA

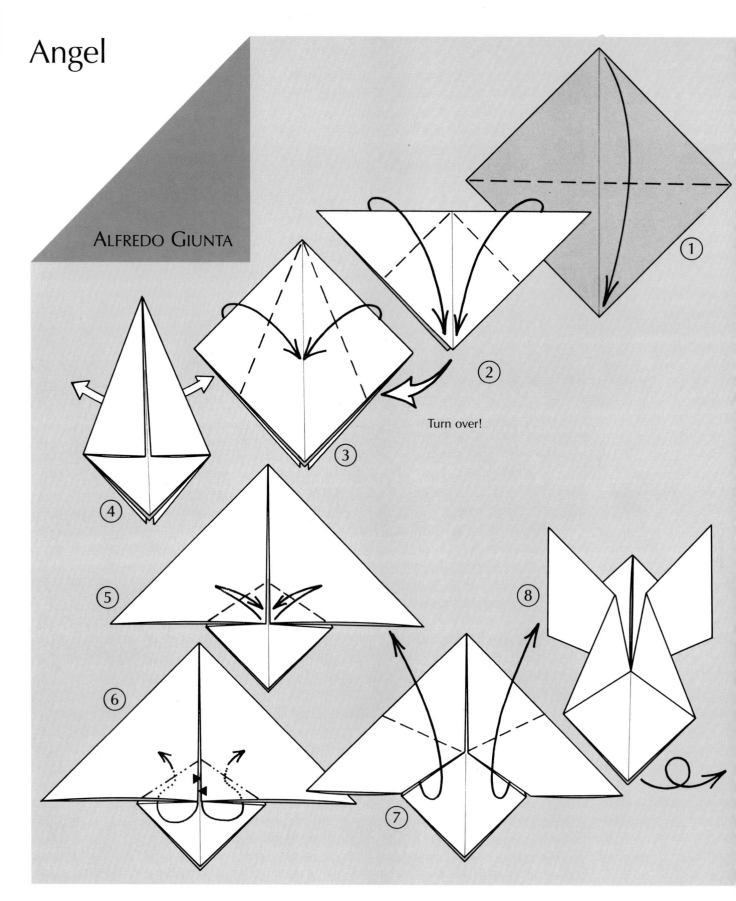

Turn over!

Valley fold the creases for the wing from the back of the model. They are optional and serve to curve the wing.

⑨

⑩

⑪

⑫

⑬

65

Decoration

SAM CUILLA

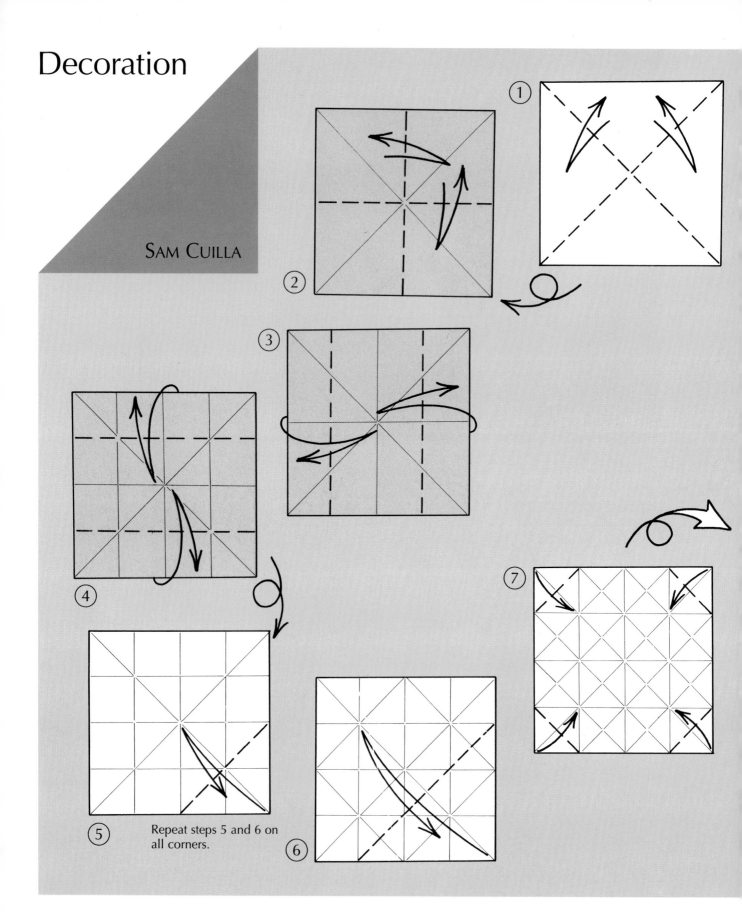

Repeat steps 5 and 6 on all corners.

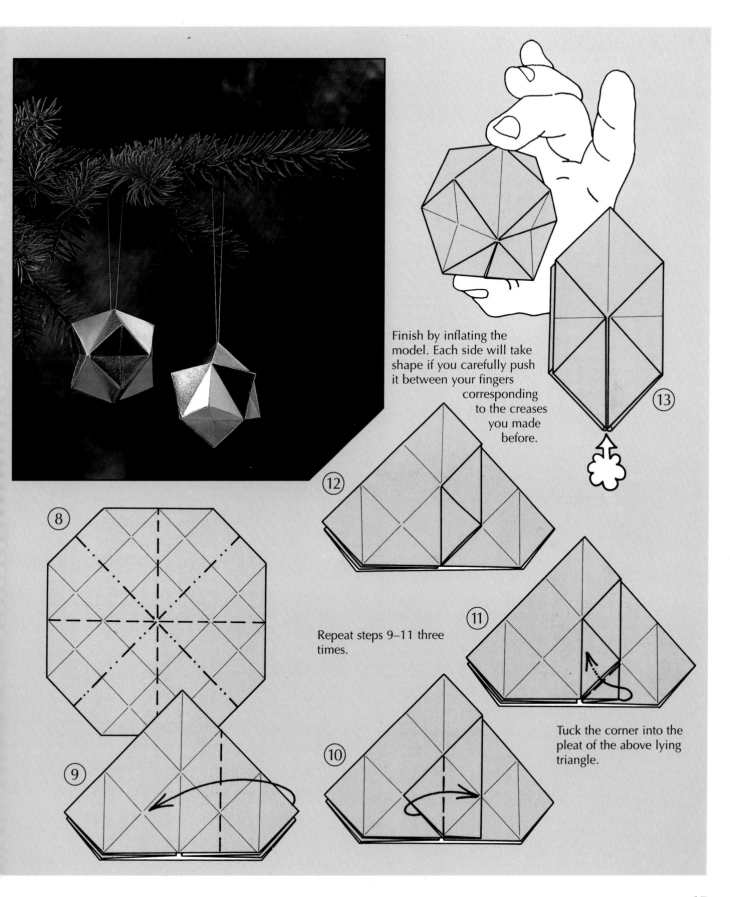

Finish by inflating the model. Each side will take shape if you carefully push it between your fingers corresponding to the creases you made before.

⑬

⑫

Repeat steps 9–11 three times.

⑪

Tuck the corner into the pleat of the above lying triangle.

⑧

⑨

⑩

Happy Santa

JOHN SMITH

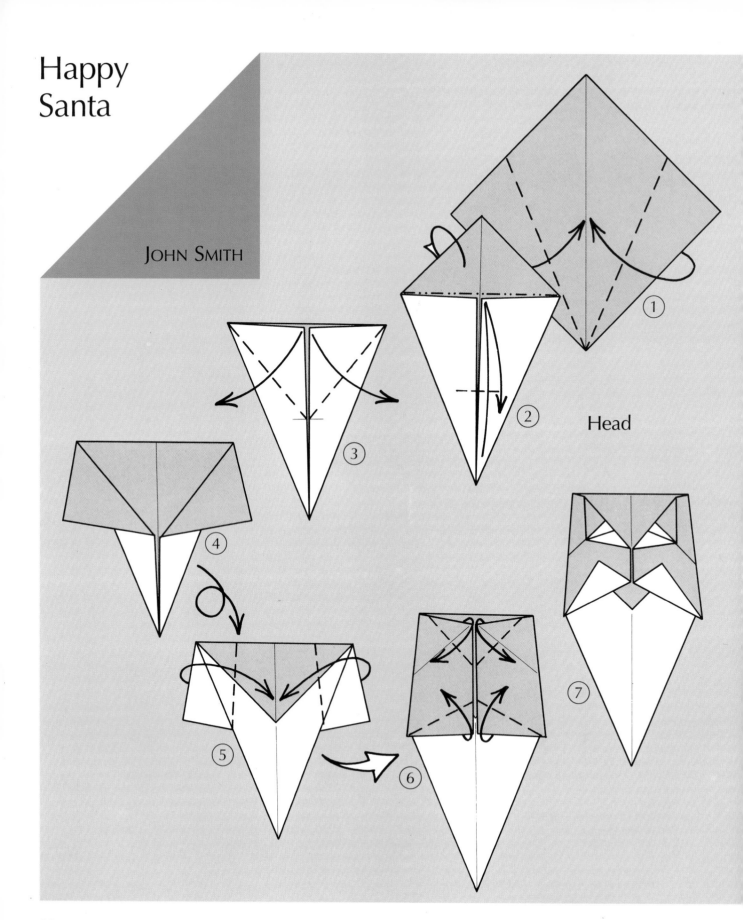

Head

John Smith has developed many models using only mountain and valley folds. By using only these two types of folds he created a series of simple models to which he gave the term "Pureland Origami". This Happy Santa was designed by John Smith in 1991 for his personal Christmas card.

Hat

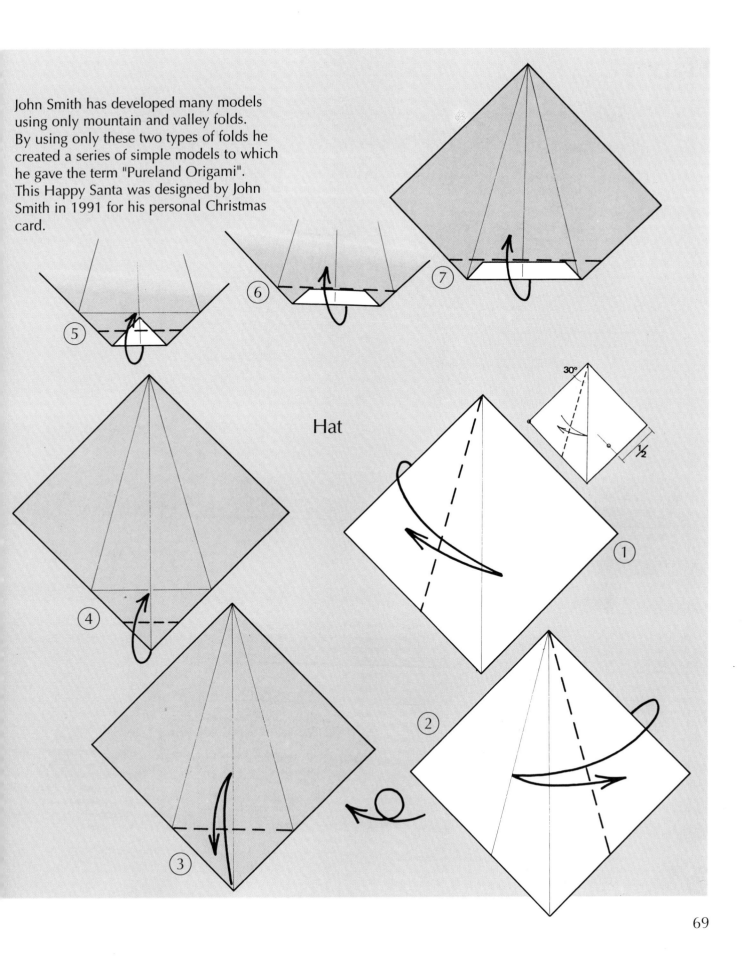

69

Geometric
Figures

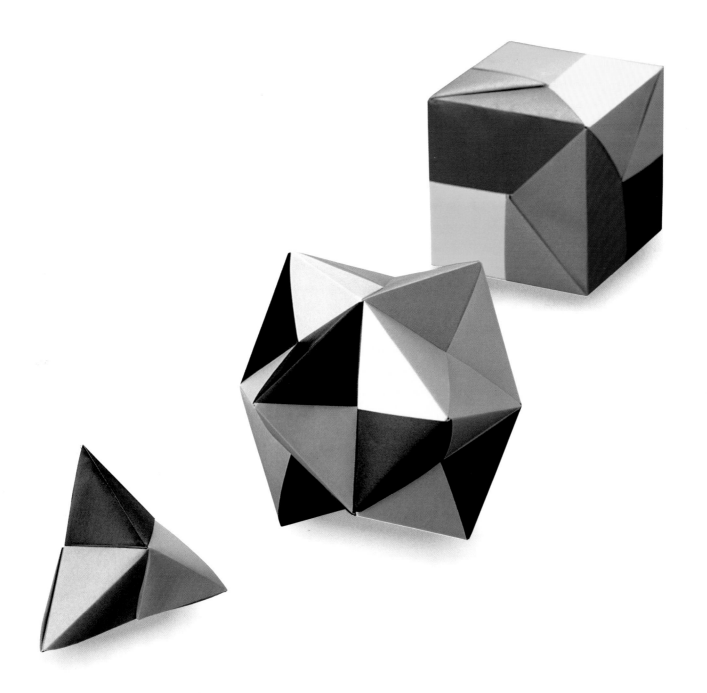

Cube

TOMOKO FUSE

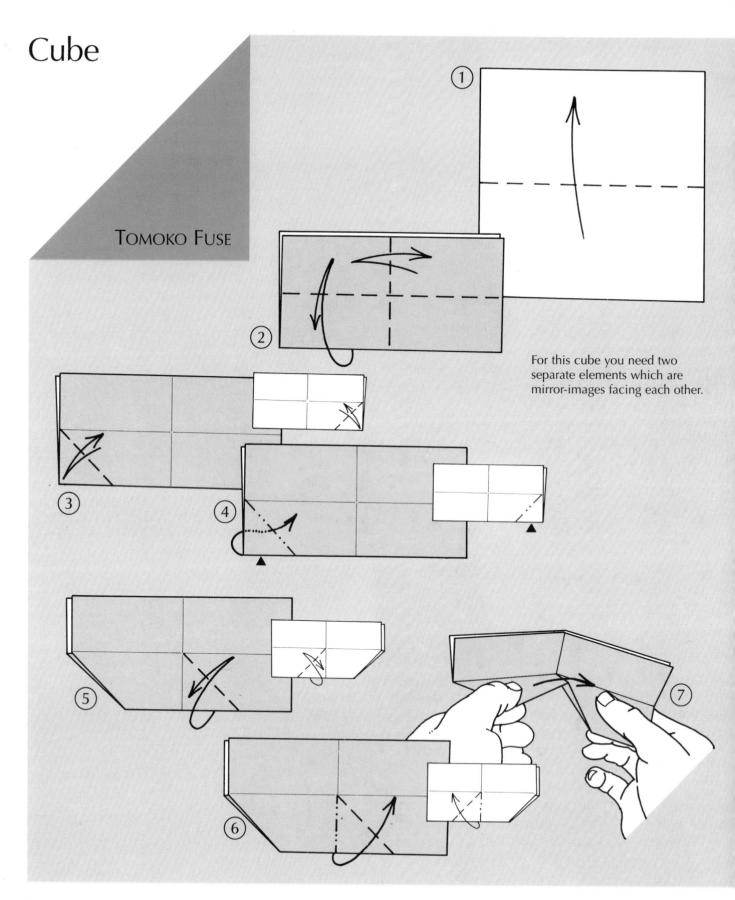

For this cube you need two separate elements which are mirror-images facing each other.

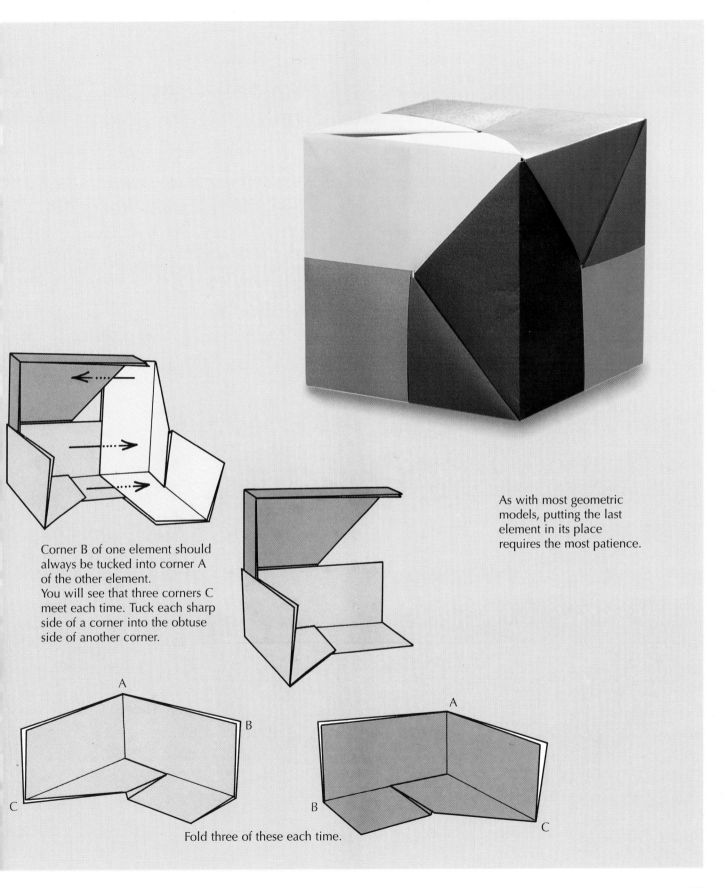

Corner B of one element should always be tucked into corner A of the other element.
You will see that three corners C meet each time. Tuck each sharp side of a corner into the obtuse side of another corner.

As with most geometric models, putting the last element in its place requires the most patience.

Fold three of these each time.

Open Cube

Tomoko Fuse

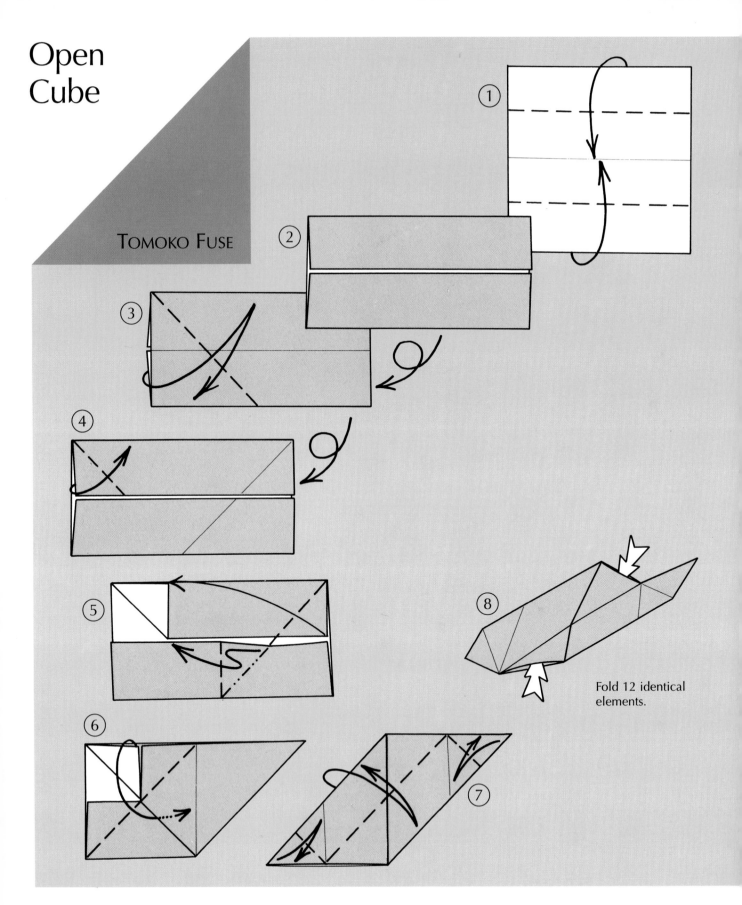

Fold 12 identical elements.

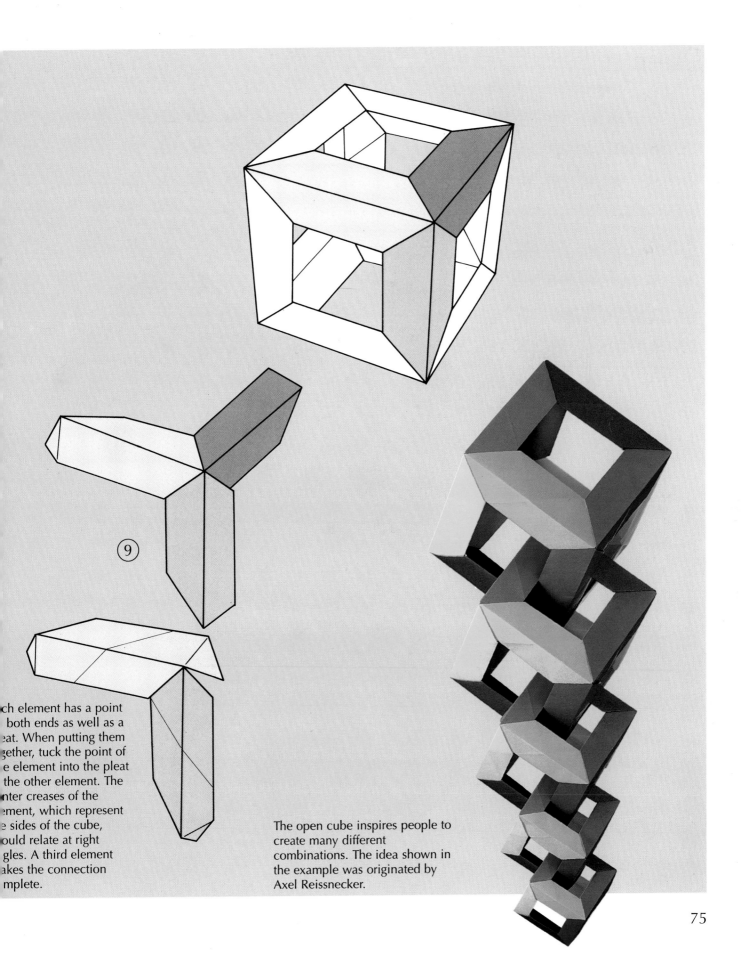

(9)

ch element has a point
both ends as well as a
eat. When putting them
gether, tuck the point of
e element into the pleat
the other element. The
nter creases of the
ement, which represent
e sides of the cube,
ould relate at right
gles. A third element
akes the connection
mplete.

The open cube inspires people to
create many different
combinations. The idea shown in
the example was originated by
Axel Reissnecker.

75

Sonobe Cube

MITSUNOBU SONOBE

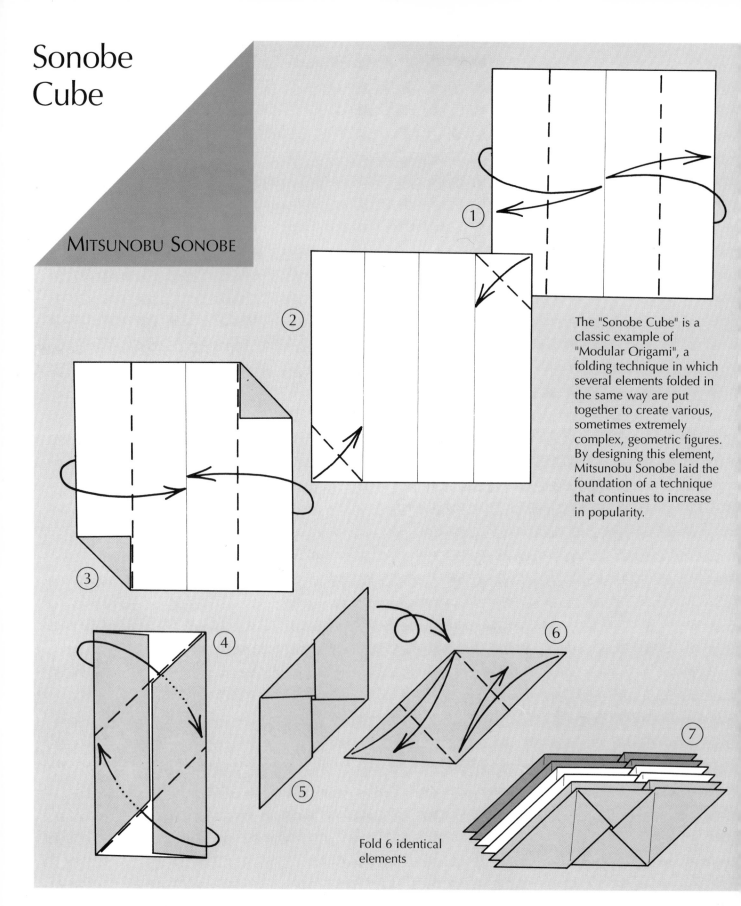

The "Sonobe Cube" is a classic example of "Modular Origami", a folding technique in which several elements folded in the same way are put together to create various, sometimes extremely complex, geometric figures. By designing this element, Mitsunobu Sonobe laid the foundation of a technique that continues to increase in popularity.

Fold 6 identical elements

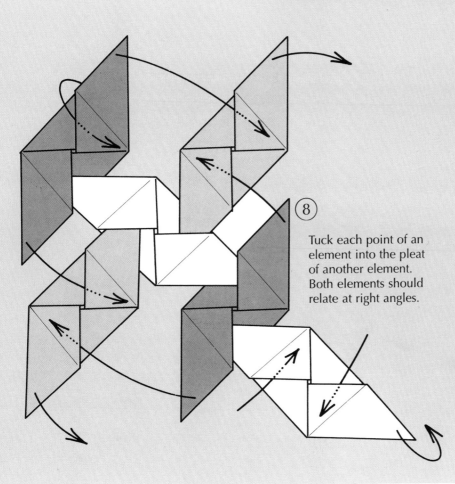

⑧

Tuck each point of an
element into the pleat
of another element.
Both elements should
relate at right angles.